OMDURMAN
1898

OMDURMAN
1898

WILLIAM WRIGHT

First published 2012 by
Spellmount, an imprint of
The History Press
The Mill, Brimscombe Port
Stroud, Gloucestershire, GL5 2QG
www.thehistorypress.co.uk

British Library Cataloguing in Publication Data.
A catalogue record for this book is available from the British Library.

ISBN 978 0 7524 6872 3

Typesetting and origination by The History Press
Printed in Great Britain

CONTENTS

ACKNOWLEDGEMENTS

First, let me thank all authors who have trod the desert sands before me and to whom I owe a debt; I especially acknowledge all those quoted in the text and thank them for their help. The illustrations are from my own collection and once again I am grateful for the care with which Krisztina Elias has re-photographed them. A big debt of gratitude to Shaun Barrington, my editor at The History Press, and the guiding light in all that I have written.

LIST OF ILLUSTRATIONS

List of Illustrations

26 Some cheerful Cameron Highlanders advancing towards Omdurman.

27 A quartet of war correspondents. Left to right: Bennet Burleigh (*Daily Telegraph*); Rene Bull, (*Black and White*); Frederic Villiers (*Illustrated London News*); and Hamilton Weldon (*Morning Post*).

28 The initial charge of the Mahdist army.

29 Kitchener observes and directs his battle from a small mound.

30 One of the gunboat crews in action on the Nile.

31 A rare photograph of Maxwell (mounted) talking with an aide just a few minutes before the initial dervish attack. Note the Egyptian troops resting or kneeling in their zariba trench.

32 A rare photograph of the 21st Lancers shortly before the famous charge, resting by the slopes of Jebel Surgham.

33 Captain Paul Kenna VC, 21st Lancers.

34 Beja friendlies – the curly-haired Hadendowa are the same tribe that slaughtered the 21st Lancers.

35 Lieutenant the Honourable Raymond de Montmorency VC, 21st Lancers.

36 The last full regimental charge of British cavalry.

37 Private Thomas Byrne VC, 21st Lancers.

38 The officers of the 21st Lancers, in a photograph taken some days after the battle. Colonel Martin is fourth from left, front row. Next to him (from left) are Majors Crole-Wyndham and Finn. Many of the men wear black armbands to commemorate their dead colleagues.

39 Lieutenant Nevill Smyth, Queen's Bays, who won a Victoria Cross saving the life of two war correspondents.

40 The heroic defence of the Khalifa's black banner.

41 Behind the firing line at Omdurman.

42 MacDonald's brigade going into action.

43 Macdonald's Sudanese repelling the vast Mahdist attack on their brigade.

44 The Battle of Omdurman – 'medieval warriors against Maxims'. (*The Illustrated London News*)

INTRODUCTION

No battle demonstrates the apex of imperial expansion by western powers up to 1900, the end of eighteenth- and nineteenth-century European warfare, the inevitable clash of modern technology with medieval-style armies, or local tribesmen hurling themselves at invading 'infidel' foreigners quite so well as Omdurman, 2 September 1898. Over the years several misconceptions have grown up around the events of that day; chief of these – inspired by the obvious inequality of warriors armed only with spears, hurling themselves in massed attacks against well-armed, well-trained troops using dum-dum bullets, heavy artillery and machine guns – is that the Mahdists were just a rabble without any coherent plan of attack. This is not true; the dervishes had been fighting the British for 15 years and developed proven and successful methods of campaigning.

At Omdurman the Khalifa Abdullahi and his commanders had a plan. It failed for three main reasons: firstly, it required precision timing; secondly, it failed sufficiently to take into account the possible reactions of the enemy; and thirdly, it lamentably overlooked the huge technological supremacy of the Anglo-Egyptians, especially their fast-action Maxim machine guns.

Coming during the high noon of the British Empire, just after Queen Victoria's Diamond Jubilee, the Battle of Omdurman was hugely popular amongst all classes of British society. The Press crowed that it liberated the Sudan, ended the tyrannical rule of the Khalifa, revenged the death of General Gordon in 1885 and expunged the national shame caused by the withdrawal from the Sudan. Politicians were delighted that Omdurman helped confirm British domination of the Nile valley to its uppermost reaches while removing the Mahdist threat for a moderate cost in men and money.

The Press made a media star out of the relatively unknown commander of the Egyptian Army chosen to plan and lead the advance to Omdurman – Horatio Herbert Kitchener, the Sirdar. This somewhat cold and aloof man would rise meteorically to become, by the time of the battle, more famous than most other Victorian generals. Kitchener was a poor tactician and the battle would display weaknesses in him and even worse ones in his opponent. Yet Kitchener's carefully planned, methodical re-conquest of the Sudan, which he always hoped would end in a battle outside Omdurman (the Mahdist capital) was and remains a magnificent example of good logistical planning.

In an age when fundamentalist warriors were just as prevalent as today, the Battle of Omdurman destroyed the Mahdiya and its attempts at global *jihad*. Now, in the twenty-first century, when British soldiers still face Muslim fundamentalists on the battlefield, fighting across inhospitable terrain, Kitchener's strategy, the remarkable achievements of his spymaster, Reginald Wingate, along with the battle itself, can give much food for thought for soldiers and armchair historians alike.

TIMELINE

1881	12 August	Mahdists defeat Egyptians on Aba Island. *Jihad* proclaimed by Mahdi
1883	5 November	Hicks Pasha's army wiped out at Sheikan
1885	26 January	Fall of Khartoum and death of Gordon
	31 December	Battle of Ginniss
1888	3 August	Mahdist invasion of Egypt defeated at Battle of Toski
1896	1 March	Abyssinians defeat Italians at Battle of Adowa
	12 March	Britain agrees to re-invade Dongola province, Sudan
	15 March	Hunter leads Egyptian troops to Akasha
	7 June	Battle of Firka
	19 September	Artillery duel at Hafir
	23 September	Anglo-Egyptian troops enter Dongola
1897	1 January	First track laid at Wady Halfa on Sudan Military Railway line to Abu Hamed
	7 August	Battle of Abu Hamed
	31 August	Kitchener occupies Berber
	31 October	Railway reaches Abu Hamed

Timeline

1898

1 January	Kitchener asks for British troop reinforcements
16 February	Anglo-Egyptian Army concentrates at Kenur
30 March	General Hunter reconnoitres Mahmud's zareba
4 April	Second reconnaissance, Broadwood's cavalry action
8th April	Battle of the Atbara
18 August	Final troops leave Atbara for the front
28 August	Concentration of the Anglo-Egyptian Army at Jebel Royan for final battle
31 August	Kerreri reconnoitred and shelled
1 September	Omdurman reconnoitred, forts silenced, Mahdists make preparations for battle
2 September	Battle of Omdurman and capture of city
4 September	Gordon memorial service held at Khartoum
9 September	Kitchener starts up Nile to meet French at Fashoda
22 September	Battle of Gedaref
24 September	Sirdar returns from Fashoda

1899

24 November	Action of Um Dibaykarat and death of the Khalifa Abdullahi

HISTORICAL BACKGROUND

The Rise of the Mahdi

The astonishing man who was – for a short time – to humble Britain, was a boat builder's son, born on 12 August 1844 at Dongola, a dismal provincial crossroads on the Nile. Twenty-five years earlier the Egyptian ruler, Muhammad Ali Pasha, had invaded and conquered much of the Sudan in the name of his overlord, the Turkish Sultan. Egyptian rule was to be marked by sloth, corruption and oppression.

At the age of five Muhammad Ahmed's family moved to Omdurman and the boy started attending a religious school in Khartoum. He was an intensely devout scholar who studied Arabic, mathematics and astronomy as well as theology. Within a few years his piety was obvious and he grew increasingly ascetic, studying Sufi mysticism. Ahmed then moved to the island of Aba, which lies on the White Nile, 160 miles south of Khartoum, and urged his brothers to join him. Living as a hermit in a cave by the Nile, his holy reputation grew.

'Devote yourselves to God and abstain from worldly pleasures,' he preached, 'This world is for infidels'; Ahmed's 'infidels' were the corrupt Egyptian government officials and their hated soldiers. An early adherent to his teaching was a young man of the Baggara

1. Muhammad Ahmed el-Sayyid Abdullah – the Mahdi of Allah – the greatest fundamentalist Muslim warrior of the nineteenth century.

tribe called Abdullahi al-Taishi. From the start the two men got along and realised each had qualities that the other lacked. Muhammad Ahmed was 'a prophet and a preacher; a saint and a visionary; a man who could inspire and charm; one whose own fervour and conviction could make men follow wherever he led,' while Abdullahi was 'a man of action and affairs; a fighter and an administrator; one who combined a ruthless strength of will with a quick intelligence, and who had the force to translate theories into action. Where the one could inspire devotion, the other compelled obedience.' The movement thus got a saint and enforcer.

Formulating his thoughts and religious philosophy, Mohammad Ahmed gradually came to the conclusion that he was the *Mahdi al-Muntazar* (literally 'he who is guided aright'), the man destined to bring righteousness to an imperfect world. Soon he was starting to preach *jihad*, or holy war, against unbelievers. This was too much for the Sudan governor, Rauf Pasha, who sent two companies of soldiers to Aba to seize the self-styled 'Mahdi' and bring him to Khartoum in chains. The troops arrived at night and stumbled ashore where they were surprised by a yelling crowd of Muhammad Ahmed's supporters. Before they could even fire

their weapons, 120 soldiers were dead and only a few got back to Khartoum alive. The great Mahdist War had begun.

For the next 20 months the Mahdists scored an almost unbroken run of successes against a bewildered, out-manoeuvred and increasingly terrified Egyptian administration. These victories were helped enormously in 1882 by the fact that Egypt itself was in ferment as the British invaded to defeat a nationalist government. On 13 September, at Tel-el-Kebir in the desert near Alexandria, the Egyptian Army under Arabi Pasha was defeated by the Anglo-Indian forces of Major-General Sir Garnet Wolseley. Britain was now stuck with what the popular Press called 'Gladstone's egg'. Meanwhile the Mahdi's followers – known as dervishes – had speedily created an efficient fighting machine and on 19 January 1883 seized the garrison town of El Obeid and its arsenal of 6000 Remington rifles.

In April the dervish army, or *ansar*, got its first bloody nose when 4000 of them were killed at al-Marasi, an early foretaste of Omdurman. The enemy commander – who divided his forces into land and river units, cunningly placed his artillery along the likely line of a dervish retreat and cut off another escape route by burning the dervishes' rafts – was an Indian Army colonel, with the local rank of major-general, William Hicks. With fierce eyes, a goatee beard and thick moustache, Hicks was an officer of the old school who expected his soldiers to be as disciplined as he was. Unfortunately his troops were of indifferent quality, his officers arguably worse, his chain of command unclear and he himself was impatient, indecisive, obstinate and undiplomatic. That summer he led his army into the baking hot wastes of Kordofan to the west of Khartoum, looking for the Mahdi. The whole campaign was a fiasco of mismanagement as Hicks was drawn deeper and deeper into the desert. Then, on 5 November, after prayers, the Mahdi told the ansar: 'You will kill this expedition in less than half an hour.' He was right. Exhausted, too weak to resist and dying of thirst, Hicks' 10,000-strong army was wiped out in the thorn forest of Sheikan. He died gallantly and his head was cut off and sent to the Mahdi.

Things got worse; in December a force of Egyptian gendarmerie (some in leg irons after resisting being sent to the Sudan) arrived in Suakin on the Red Sea coast. Their commander, a disgraced British officer, Valentine Baker Pasha, was ordered to 'act with the greatest prudence', but he hankered for glory and a chance to redeem his honour. Near the desert wells of El Teb on 4 February 1884 the dervishes, under a wily leader called Osman Digna (soon to become known as the best of the Mahdist generals), were waiting. Their surprise attack panicked the Egyptians who turned and ran. With ease the ansar killed 96 officers and 2225 men, capturing 4 Krupp cannon, 3000 rifles and 500,000 rounds of ammunition.

The British get Involved

Desert garrisons such as Sinkat were also attacked by the Mahdists and lost. Into this deteriorating situation came Major-General Sir Gerald Graham VC, who landed at Suakin with 3000 British troops and gave the dervishes a sharp lesson at the Second Battle of El Teb. On 14 March he slaughtered 2000 more of them at Tamai (with a loss of 221 killed and wounded), but not before, in Kipling's words, the dervishes 'bruk a British square'.

Some 24,000 Egyptian troops were left scattered in lonely Sudanese outposts. After the defeat of Hicks, the British government had agreed that the Sudan had to be abandoned.

IN THE SHADE

One of the oddest innovations planned for the 1884–85 Sudan Expedition was an order for 10,000 umbrellas! The idea was that these shades would combat sunstroke. The weirdly comic sight of regiments of British soldiers marching along under their umbrellas never materialised, as they did not arrive in time, so the order was rescinded.

But who was to extricate the remaining troops and citizens? A journalist, W.T. Stead, thought he had the answer. In his influential journal, *The Pall Mall Gazette*, he ran an interview under the headline, 'Gordon for the Sudan'. It was a clever ploy because his champion was already a household name, thought by many to be a mix of modern crusader and soldier-saint – Charles George Gordon. He had seen action in the Crimean War and also led a vast army against the Taiping rebels in China armed only with a cane. His friends labelled him courageous and intelligent; his enemies said he was eccentric and highly unpredictable; the public loved him. In Cairo the British representative, Sir Evelyn Baring, the most powerful man in the country, who had met Gordon during an earlier stint in the Sudan, commented drily that he doubted if he could control a man 'who habitually consults the Prophet Isaiah when he is in difficulty.'

In Cairo the new Governor-General of the Sudan made it clear that he had his own plans for the country rather more elaborate than those of the British government. Baring tried to help but thought Gordon 'half-cracked'. Arriving in Khartoum on 18 February, Gordon burned all the tax records and told the locals, 'I come without soldiers, but with God on my side.' Gordon tried to bribe the Mahdi and sent him a beautiful robe; Muhammad Ahmed sent it back with a charming letter, and a dervish white cotton patched shirt, or *jibbah*. Both men realised they were equally dogmatic and incorruptible.

Gordon Relief Expedition

Gradually the Mahdists encircled Khartoum; in the city with Gordon were 25,000 civilians and 8000 soldiers. On 26 May Berber fell and the city was finally cut off. Meantime in London the government was still procrastinating about sending help; Prime Minister Gladstone objected to 'a war of conquest against a people struggling to be free'. Baring in Cairo warned that Gordon could not be left stranded, 'if, from a military point of view, it is at

2. Gordon's Last Stand *by G.W. Joy, one of the most evocative imperialist paintings.*

all possible to help him.' Finally, in August, a relief expedition was organised under Wolseley; the original 'modern major-general' of Gilbertian wit, his highly unorthodox campaign combined British infantry with skilled boatmen from Canada and West Africa, volunteer units from Australia and the hurried formation and training of four camel regiments. This Desert Column was to be assisted by a River Column in the final phase. The new Egyptian Army was given the task of guarding the lines of communication. Wolseley decided against constructing a railway line from Suakin to Berber, with a final dash across the desert towards Khartoum in favour of the longer, slower but safer Nile route.

On 28 January 1885, huddled on board the steamer *Bordein* as it approached the confluence of the Blue and White Niles at Khartoum, were two British army officers, Sir Charles Wilson and

Captain Fred Gascoigne, with 10 non-commissioned officers and men of the Royal Sussex Regiment and 110 Sudanese soldiers. Not far behind was a sister ship, the *Talahawiyeh*, where a similar compliment of British troops and 80 more Sudanese also knelt behind the improvised protection of boiler plates and sandbags.

Their Nile journey had been perilous, as was their mission to rescue Gordon. 'The bullets began to fly pretty quickly, tapping like hail against the ship's sides, whilst the shells went screeching overhead or threw jets of water in the stream round us,' Wilson later recalled. From Omdurman on the opposite bank of the Nile, 'Two or more guns opened upon us … and three or four from Khartoum … the roll of musketry from each side was continuous; and high above that could be heard … the loud rushing noise of the Krupp shells.' Masses of the enemy, with banners fluttering in the breeze, lined the river bank near what had been Gordon's palace. 'No flag was flying in Khartoum and not a shot was fired in our assistance,' wrote Wilson, who felt he suffered a 'crushing' blow. 'May God have mercy on me, but this is enough to drive most men mad,' wrote General Lord Wolseley. Back home, Queen Victoria, literally made ill by events, blamed Prime Minister Gladstone, '& it is I who have, as the Head of the Nation, to bear the tragic humiliation.'

The perilous river journey was all for nothing. Gordon had refused every chance of escape (he had earlier declined an offer of safe passage from the Mahdi). He used all his skills as a Royal Engineer to defend Khartoum and died bravely there during the Mahdist attack on 26 January. He had held out for 317 days. Wilson in *Bordein* arrived just two days late. It would have been Gordon's 52nd birthday.

The rescue force withdrew, the dervishes keeping up their attacks; at Kirbekan on 10 February 1885 they shot dead the River Column commander, having already slain the Desert Column leader, thus notching up both generals as kills (not forgetting Gordon and Hicks). Quite an impressive achievement. Back in Cairo the Desert Column's 34-year-old intelligence officer, Major

3. 'Too Late' by John Tenniel, Punch, 14 February 1885. This cartoon encapsulated a nation's humiliation at the death of Gordon and fall of Khartoum.

Kitchener, wrote privately that 'the organisation of the Expedition has been very bad' and vowed to avenge the death of his hero and fellow Royal Engineer. He wrote to his family: 'The shock of the news was dreadful, and I can hardly realise it yet.'

Khalifa Abdullahi Assumes Power

On 22 June 1885 the Mahdi died suddenly of a severe fever, most likely typhus (though poison and meningitis have also been suggested). He died in a spartan bed in his simple quarters, a shed made from the boards of General Hicks' stable. On his death bed he declared Abdullahi, one of his three *khalifas*, or chief lieutenants, as his successor. A very different kind of man, the new ruler of the Sudan moved quickly to enlarge his personal power base: influential figures who might transfer allegiance from the Mahdi to one of the two other khalifas were reduced in rank, banished or killed; the Mahdi's sons and family, known as the *ashraf*, were marginalised; and new powers were given to his own brother, Yaqub, and his loyal Baggara tribesmen. Just four weeks after the Mahdi's death Abdullahi flexed his muscles and ordered the entire population of Khartoum to move. Detesting the city, which he associated with 'Turks' and foreigners, Khartoum was soon a ghost town as its armouries, boatyards, factories and workshops were replicated in Omdurman.

The ansar harassed the retreating British almost to the Egyptian border; however, on 30 December they were caught off-guard in a dawn attack by troops under the command of General Sir Frederick Stephenson, C-in-C of the British Army of Occupation. The Battle of Ginnis saw some fierce close-quarter fighting; William Butler, commanding one of the brigades, thought it a 'strange sight' as the dervishes hacked with medieval-style swords. In a foretaste of the Battle of Omdurman, he was impressed how they fell, 'their faces distorted with the delirium of fanatical enthusiasm, the lips moving in prayer, the eyes rolling, their swords raised in both hands … I could not discern any sign of rage in the expression of their faces; it seemed to me be the ecstasy of self-martyrdom.'

Rebirth of the Egyptian Army

Officially the Battle of Ginnis was fought by the new Anglo-Egyptian Frontier Field Force but it was, in reality, the last conflict of the 1884–85 war. Both sides needed time to lick their wounds. Writing on the day after the battle, Stephenson commented on the 'excellent behaviour' of the Egyptian troops who had been 'very steady under fire and fought in line side by side with English.' The four guns captured in the battle were the work of Egyptian troops. Joscelin Wodehouse, commanding the Egyptian artillery, had actually charged into the dervish camp shouting, 'Don't let the English get the flags!' as he tried to pick up enemy banners as trophies for his gunners and other Egyptian corps.

The important task of reorganising the Egyptian Army had begun as soon as the 1882 war had drawn to a close. One of Wolseley's circle, Major-General Sir Evelyn Wood VC, was tasked with training and equipping a new force of 6000 men within a budget of £200,000. This sum included the salaries of 25 British officers (on rates of pay higher than in the British Army), who were to be its core. Each officer had to have a first-class military record with proven ability in horsemanship and musketry. They also had to learn Arabic, be able to give commands in German and handle official correspondence in French. Their old British ranks were stepped up with none holding a rank lower than major. Contracts were for two years and leave, like pay, was generous. Native Egyptians were also encouraged to strive for commissions and several did.

In the summer of 1883 a severe cholera outbreak ravaged Egypt. The Egyptian Army Medical Service had barely been formed so the new officers had to act as medical orderlies. The care and attention they showed to their sick and dying soldiers helped create an association and comradeship that was, as one officer wrote, 'very remarkable'. It was the kernel of an Egyptian *esprit de corps*.

SIR EVELYN WOOD VC

The first Sirdar of the new Egyptian Army had a reputation for being one of the most clumsy officers of all time! He once fell off a giraffe, suffering holes through both cheeks and a crushed nose, was wounded in the arm in the Crimea, got shot by West African natives with a nail gun and tripped out of a carriage in South Africa, causing his feet to swell up like footballs. Notoriously half-deaf, an aide once said it was necessary to 'carry a chemist's shop', just to treat all his ailments.

THE OLD WAYS

Part of the problem for the conscripts in the old Egyptian Army was their curious method of pay. Corrupt government officials often stole their money and made the soldiers take payments in lengths of cloth. The poor men then had to sell these to merchants at a fraction of their official value. Cloth was sold back to government officials at a profit and so this corrupt ring of circumstances benefitted everyone except the soldiers.

Despite some language difficulties at first, as well as a small mutiny, the new Egyptian Army quickly started to develop into a fighting machine. Happily the non-commissioned officers and men showed a rare fondness for drill combined with high levels of stamina and endurance. By the early 1890s an officer noted:

> The present army are well fed, well paid and well clothed. They get periodical furloughs to see their friends; are allowed … to travel by train or steamer at greatly reduced rates; are given medals for active service; and if discharged from the service on account of wounds or sickness, they are sent home with a gratuity and a complete set of clothes.

The new Egyptian Army finally had a chance to show its worth at Toski in 1889 when the Khalifa Abdullahi sent one of his rivals, the Emir Wad al-Nejumi, on what was in essence a suicide mission to invade Egypt. That June al-Nejumi had been at Sarras with 6000 fighters and 8000 followers. In July, part of his force was headed off from the river at Argin by Colonel J. Wodehouse and lost 1400 men, dead or captured. In August, in a replay of Hicks' defeat at Sheikan, but in reverse, the starved yet brave ansar were checked by a larger Egyptian force under the Sirdar (commander in chief) Sir Francis Grenfell who cleverly brought his enemy to battle on open ground where his artillery and machine guns could create

---

A CAN OF WORMS

Officers joining the new Egyptian Army were a highly spirited lot but none more so than Charles Chamley Turner who, in an age of high jinks, was crazier than most. A friend once gave him a box full of venomous snakes on the terrace of Shepheard's Hotel in Cairo. With delight Turner held up a clutch of the deadly reptiles, waving them around and shouting, 'Snakes! Oh ripping!' Tables overturned and women screamed as Turner calmly flung them into the street. It was only later that he asked his friend if they had been poisonous.

---

most havoc. Over 1200 dervishes were killed and 4000 taken prisoner. Wad al-Nejumi and his five-year-old son were found dead side by side on the battlefield.

This was Abdullahi's only attempt to invade Egypt. But on the Red Sea coast Osman Digna never gave up being a menace. At Handub in 1888 Kitchener tried to surprise the dervish base but was wounded in the jaw during a counter-attack. More battles took place in the Eastern Sudan at Gemaizeh and Tokar in December 1888 and February 1891. The new British Prime Minister, Lord Salisbury, viewed these encounters with caution and told Baring that soldiers 'would insist on the importance of garrisoning the moon in order to protect us from Mars.'

In 1892 Grenfell left Egypt and to everyone's surprise Kitchener, who was not popular, was made Sirdar. Four years earlier he had met Salisbury and rashly confessed that if he was ever made commander in chief he would try and re-take Khartoum. One of his later aides, Lord Edward Cecil, a son of the Prime Minister, noted how 'Comfort, affections, personalities, all were quite inferior considerations … He felt he was defrauding the Almighty if he did not carry out his task.'

THE ARMIES

The Anglo-Egyptian Commanders

Sirdar (C-In-C) Major-General Sir H.H. Kitchener

Born into an Anglo-Irish military family, Kitchener entered the Royal Military Academy at Woolwich in 1867, where he met his lifelong hero, Charles Gordon. In 1870 he served as a volunteer with a French field ambulance in the Franco-Prussian War. Eleven years later he went on spying missions during the early stages of the Egyptian War. His abilities as an orientalist made him a natural choice as one of the first recruits to the new Egyptian Army in February 1883. After intelligence duties in 1884–85 he was made Governor-General of the Eastern Sudan (1886–88) and Adjutant-General of the Egyptian Army (1888–92) before his appointment as Sirdar.

Tall, with light brown hair parted in the middle, a wavy almost blonde moustache and blue eyes, Kitchener was an imposing figure. Brusque, dour, cold, even brutal, he made enemies easily. He was incapable of delegating even simple tasks, and could be cruel to the few staff he had. A strict routine meant that he liked to get through at least three hours of work before breakfast. His drinking was temperate, his uniform spotless and he would go

4. Major-General Sir Horatio Herbert Kitchener, painted by H. von Herkomer. As Sirdar of the Egyptian Army and Commander in Chief of the Sudan re-conquest, it fell to him to avenge Gordon's death.

into a rage if anyone touched his papers. He detested failure, weakness and even sickness in others – and himself. He also did not aim to be popular amongst the troops but in time they came to revere him.

Beneath his outward reserve Kitchener felt the pressures of what he was expected to achieve. 'You have no idea what continual anxiety, worry and strain I have through it all,' he told a friend in 1897. Those working closely with him had mixed opinions; Hunter (see below) once raged that his superior was 'inhuman, heartless with eccentric and freakish bursts of generosity ... a vain, egotistical mass of pride and ambition, expecting and usurping all and giving nothing.'

Both the Consul-General in Cairo, Sir Evelyn Baring (raised to Lord Cromer in 1892) and Lord Salisbury in London respected a soldier who 'did not think that extravagance was the handmaid of efficiency', though one biographer has said that Kitchener 'accepted the need for parsimony with a whole heartedness which suggested at least a measure of relish.' His training as an engineer allowed him full rein on the campaign to work out his superb logistical organisation of supply and transport. Aloof, intelligent, over-seeing all and divulging only what he thought necessary, men praised him as an automaton. The *Daily Mail* correspondent G.W. Steevens felt Kitchener 'ought to be patented and shown with pride at the Paris International Exhibition. British Empire, Exhibit No. 1, *hors concours*, the Sudan Machine.'

Major-General Sir W.F. Gatacre

The commander of the British Infantry Division was a 55-year-old martinet who had served previously in the Hazara Expedition of 1888 and Chitral Relief Expedition both on India's north-west frontier. Known to the troops as 'Backacher', because of

5. Major-General Sir William Gatacre, the unpopular commander of the British Infantry Division.

his fondness for drill, Gatacre was 'universally unpopular' with Tommies and fellow officers alike, though Kitchener admired his perfectionism and said he was 'just the right man for the job.' A subaltern writing home disagreed and said Gatacre was 'a gasbag ... who talked drivel ... and would make a splendid corporal ... the general opinion is that he ought to be locked up.' Neville Lyttelton, who commanded one of the two brigades under Gatacre, fairly summed him up as 'brave as a lion, and I never came across such restless and untiring energy. No day was too hot for him, no hours too long, no work too hard. But he was very very jealous of authority, he wanted to do everything himself, and was very fond of the sound of his own voice.'

Colonel (Acting Brigadier-General) A.G. Wauchope

Wauchope was a 53-year-old Scot who commanded the 1st British Brigade and had made a habit of getting wounded in battle. He had seen action during the Ashanti War 1874, at Tel-el-Kebir and against Osman Digna in the eastern Sudan in 1884–85, on each occasion with his beloved Black Watch Regiment. Lyttelton thought he was 'the direct opposite of Gatacre, equally brave, but very quiet and reserved. It was amusing to see him listening to Gatacre's harangues, looking pensively at him with a far-away gaze as if he saw something through and beyond him.'

6. Colonel (acting Brigadier-General) Andy Wauchope, the intensely Scottish commander of the 1st British Brigade.

Colonel (Acting Brigadier-General) N.G. Lyttelton

The commander of the 2nd British Brigade was a relative of Gladstone and considered one of the rising brains in the British Army. The 52-year-old had fought the Fenians in Canada as a young officer and later served on the staff of the 1882 Egyptian Expedition. He would become Commander-in-Chief, South Africa, 1902–1904 and then Chief of Staff and First Military Member of the Army Council, 1904–1908. He was appointed Governor of the Royal hospital, Chelsea, in 1912, where he died in 1931.

7. Colonel (acting Brigadier-General) Neville Lyttelton, the cool and perceptive commander of the 2nd British Brigade.

Lieutenant-Colonel R.H. Martin

Martin commanded the 21st Lancers, the only British cavalry regiment at Omdurman. After several years peacetime service in India, it was the 50-year-old officer's first campaign. One of Kitchener's staff officers described Martin as 'sharp, active and keen'.

Colonel C.J. Long

Long commanded the British and Egyptian artillery at Omdurman. He was a 49-year-old gunner with experience of fighting the Afghans in 1879–80, reckoned to be equally brave, impetuous and 'slow of speech'.

Commander C. Keppel RN

This Royal Navy officer led the flotilla of ten gunboats at Omdurman from the *Zafir*. Other officers included Lieutenant W.H. Cowan RN on *Sultan* and Lieutenant D. Beatty RN on *Fatteh*; all three later becoming admirals. Also on *Zafir* was Brev-Major Prince Christian Victor of Schleswig-Holstein, an officer of the aristocratic 60th Rifles and a grandson of the Queen.

El Lewa (Major-General) A. Hunter

The commander of the Egyptian and Sudanese troops was described as 'Kitchener's sword-arm'. The dapper and dainty Archie Hunter was second-in-command of the Egyptian Army and thus the Sirdar's deputy. A lowland Scot (though actually born in London), 41-year-old Hunter had joined the British Army at seventeen. Bored by peacetime soldiering and with no patron he had been delighted to join the Egyptian Army in 1884. 'Hooray' was how he took the news of the re-conquest, 'Never was so pleased in all my life. The men are all in grand fighting trim.' A fellow officer described him as 'a real live Cromwellian, brutal, cruel, licentious, religious, brave, able, blunt and cunning.' He was a no-nonsense soldier, devoted to his service, a realist who had a tendency to foolishly speak his mind at times, a man's man who thought nothing of taking his Abyssinian mistress with him to Cairo.

8. El Lewa
(Major-General)
Archibald Hunter, the
energetic and ruthless
field commander of the
Egyptian Army.

El Miralai (Colonel) H.A. MacDonald

'Fighting Mac' was the 45-year-old commander of the 1st Brigade, Egyptian Division. A Highland crofter's son who had risen through the ranks as a result of his bravery and the patronage of Field-Marshal Lord Roberts, he had slogged from Kabul to Kandahar in a famous march of the Second Afghan War, then fought on Majuba Hill against the Boers in 1881 before joining the Egyptian Army in 1885. He had commanded the 11th Sudanese at Toski and the 2nd Brigade during the Dongola campaign. G.W. Steevens described him as 'so sturdily built that you might imagine him to be armour-plated,' but another journalist, T.P. O'Connor, displaying perhaps the class bias which dogged MacDonald all his life, said: 'He was one of those men who ought never to have appeared out of uniform. He gave you the idea of strength and splendid manliness and bulldog power, but there was nothing of distinction in his air, in his manner or in his dress. He looked a Tommy in his Sunday clothes, which is not Tommy at his best.' Officers serving under MacDonald found him to be as tough as old boots and no one doubted his guts on the battlefield.

9. El Miralai (Colonel) Hector Macdonald, the immensely popular, tough ex-ranker commanding the 1st Brigade, Egyptian Division.

El Miralai (Colonel) J.G. Maxwell

Maxwell commanded the 2nd Brigade, Egyptian Division. A big man, highly regarded as an efficient soldier, he had been ADC to General Alison, commanding the Highland Brigade at Tel-el-Kebir, and served with the River Column in 1884–5 before joining the Egyptian Army. Tact was not Maxwell's strong point but he was known to be a good brigadier.

10. El Miralai (Colonel) John Maxwell, efficient commander of the 2nd Brigade, Egyptian Division.

El Miralai (Colonel) D.F. Lewis

Lewis commanded the 3rd Brigade, Egyptian Division; he had been wounded at the Siege of Eshowe during the Zulu War of 1879. Easy-going 'Taffy' was another seasoned Sudan veteran, having enlisted in the Egyptian Army in 1886.

El Miralai (Colonel) J. Collinson

Collinson had fought in Zululand and commanded the 4th Brigade, Egyptian Division, which was kept in reserve at Omdurman.

El Miralai (Colonel) R.G. Broadwood

This was the commander of the Egyptian Cavalry's first campaign. The youngest of the commanders at 36 years, Broadwood had been promoted during the Dongola Expedition. He was well liked, a long-legged, dashing soldier whom even the acerbic Douglas Haig agreed was 'a very good fellow and quite understands what the enemy and his own troops are worth.'

11. El Miralai (Colonel) Robert Broadwood who commanded the Egyptian Cavalry. He was described as 'a very good soldier and fellow too'.

Kaimakam (Lieutenant-Colonel) R.J. Tudway

Tudway commanded the eight companies of Camel Corps. Another veteran of the Sudan War 1884–5, he had fought in the desert with 'B' Company MI Camel Regiment, and had been mentioned in despatches.

The Mahdist Commanders

Khalifa Abdullahi Al-Taishi

The ruler of the Sudan was about 50 years old at the time of the re-conquest. His father and grandfather had been holy men to the nomadic Baggara, the fierce and expert horsemen of south-west Sudan. Little is known about his childhood but he was close to his two full brothers and one half-brother. There is some dispute over whether he could read or write but it is accepted that he was not a good scholar. He was a slave for a time in his twenties but regained his freedom. Many times he had dreams of a Mahdi-deliverer and was one of Muhammad Ahmed's first disciples on Aba Island. During this period he was described as being 'tall, thin, somewhat pale … with a thin pointed face and big beard.'

Gaining supreme power on the death of the Mahdi, Abdullahi centralised the Mahdist state and set up a fair legal system. Kitchener's intelligence officer Reginald Wingate, with his carefully organised propaganda, made continual sniping attacks on the Khalifa: he was growing fat by 1898, and it was said that he rarely left his house, the only two-storey one in Omdurman; he had broken the Koran and kept a harem of 400 attractive women; a huge negro was required to lift him into the saddle when he went to the mosque; and his son held orgies in his home.

Blinkered by his lack of education, believing totally in a war against apostates and unbelievers, Abdullahi was hemmed in by his own orthodoxy. In 1891 he had to defeat a plot by the Mahdi's family to overthrow him. This only increased his rule by fear. However the Khalifa was never a real dictator because the Mahdi's word was considered sacred law.

In debate it was said that Abdullahi often lacked self-confidence and needed his views reinforced by someone like his clever brother Ya'qub. It is hard to say what he might have achieved without the long wars against the British, Egyptians, Italians and Abyssinians along the Sudan's frontiers. By 1895 the Sudanese currency was virtually worthless and trade had almost stopped.

Osman Digna

The most famous Mahdist general was a native of the Diqnab tribe of the eastern Sudan. This active 47-year-old had been well educated in Islamic law, theology and astronomy. He was a Suakin merchant until corrupt government troops impounded one of his caravans. Detained for trial, he slipped away, only to be captured a second time and lose all his property. Joining the Mahdist cause,

12. A rare photograph of Osman Digna in his later years. Digna was a genius of irregular warfare who proved to be the most formidable opponent of the British in the Sudan 1883–99.

he swore allegiance and never wavered from the Mahdi or the Khalifa Abdullahi.

It could be argued that he was the greatest tactical genius of irregular desert warfare that the British Empire ever faced, a master of keeping his army cohesive, of springing surprise attacks, of hitting near the rear of a column (often its weakest point) and of knowing when to withdraw an attack (something he considered as important as when to press it home). He instinctively understood the importance of morale, telling his men that the British were fleeing when he wanted to inspire them to even greater acts of devotion. Digna was also superb at making the kind of militant speeches soldiers like to hear before a battle. These sometimes lasted five or six hours.

Despite his loyalty to the Khalifa the Emir Osman Digna was not frightened to give his opinion if he found fault with Abdullahi's instructions. His almost continual harassment of the British at Suakin for 15 years made him the most experienced of the Mahdist generals. Though he took his men to meet Kitchener at the Atbara and again at Omdurman, he was happiest in his Red Sea hills with his Beja tribesmen, Kipling's 'fuzzy-wuzzies'.

Ya'qub

The Khalifa's favourite brother and chief-of-staff was the second most powerful man in the state it was said at the time, 'Woe, woe unto him who takes on Ya'qub with evil intent.' More cunning than Abdullahi, he was responsible for internal security, and was adept at smelling out plots. In council he preferred others to express their views; later, at night in long debates, he would help his brother reach decisions. Very popular with the citizens of Omdurman, Ya'qub was charitable, the most cultured of the Khalifa's family.

Militarily he was Emir of the Black Flag and had fought at Sheikan and Khartoum, but his military judgement, like that of Abdullahi, was poor. He had no idea of the technical developments in armaments that awaited his troops on 2 September 1898.

Uthman Shaykh Al-Din

The Khalifa's favourite son commanded the Dark Green Flag at Omdurman. It was said that he had held wild parties at his home that so outraged his father that Uthman was placed under house arrest for a time. Many said the 25-year-old was charming. After the battle his home was found to contain a library of books and it seems he was one of the few Mahdists to realise there was a world beyond Sudan's frontiers. It is said that he had views on exploiting the rivalry between the European imperial powers and had talked of cooperating with France against Britain.

Never having seen action before, he was a weak choice to command the elite riflemen known as the *mulazimiyya*. Several months earlier he had started to filch the best troops and weapons from the Black Flag, but these advantages were wasted on the battlefield.

Ibrahim Al Khalil

The 24-year-old Emir led the first attack at Omdurman. Despite his youth he was the best military strategist besides Osman Digna on the Mahdist side. Bright and energetic, it was said that Ibrahim did not suffer fools gladly. Before the battle he had spent several days on ground east of the Mahdi's tomb training his men from after morning prayers until sunset. Along with Osman Digna and Osman Azrak he was one of a trio of generals who argued for a night attack on the eve of the battle, an event that might have changed history.

Osman Azrak

Born in El Obeid in 1845, Azrak had originally been a cameleer for the government postal service. His experience with mounted quadrupeds may explain why he was the only one of Abdullahi's generals to take cavalry seriously; he developed a quick, light-moving mounted ansar and refined the principle of swift attacks. He was the brains behind damaging the Anglo-Egyptian gunboat *Firka* at Hafir; when a gunner on shore missed the steamer three times Osman angrily lopped off part of the man's right hand and said he would sever his head if he missed again. The fourth shell blew up the ship's boiler. Osman returned to Omdurman after the Battle of the Atbara with just 13 men. Appreciating his courage, the Khalifa Abdullahi detached a large part of the *mulazimiyya* and made them a separate command under Osman during the battle.

Khalifa Ali Wad Helu

Commander of the Green Flag, the third Khalifa and the Mahdi's son-in-law, al-Sharif was with the Red Flag but they were not on the battlefield, despite some books asserting otherwise. Appointed by the Mahdi as his successors, with Abdullahi paramount, the three khalifas as the guardians of Mahdiism did not fight in the battle but stayed at headquarters. The Green Flag was actually led in the battle by the Emir Abdullah Abu Siwar.

The Soldiers

The British Army

8200 troops fought at Omdurman (see Order of Battle) divided into two brigades. Besides the Infantry Division under Gatacre there were two Royal Artillery field batteries and the 21st Lancers. The British infantry regiments of the time were organised into two battalions of eight 120-man companies, while the cavalry regiments had four squadrons, each with 160 men.

Soldiers enlisted in most cases for what was called 'short reserve' – a term of seven years with the colours and five years' reserve. If garrisoned abroad this changed to an additional year of active service and one less with the reserve. The British Army was a volunteer institution and there was no conscription; a private soldier was paid one shilling a day, a quartermaster-sergeant got four shillings and a major-general was paid three pounds.

The British troops in the Sudan came from all parts of the British Isles. To the ordinary Tommies it was just another bit of imperial 'foot sloggin' over Africa'. Soldiers are inveterate moaners; a typical Cameron Highlander wrote home that 'We were 42 hours on the trains, and 10 days on the barges, and it about "fed us all up". We were packed like herrings in a box and I was not sorry a bit when we finished the voyage.'

Food for the rank and file was, under the circumstances, quite good. There was a nightly allowance of rum (even though the Sirdar frowned on his men getting spirits). Private George Teigh of the Lincolns noted in his diary that on 12 June he had Norfolk

13. 'On The Highway to Khartum' by Linley Sambourne, Punch, 30 January 1897. This cartoon satirised the re-conquest with British Prime Minister Salisbury bouncing up the Nile on a camel.

dumplings for dinner and plum cake for tea while other days he could munch some sweet dates. The men thought the preserved meats were rotten so gave them to the 'friendlies' and the natives ate them with relish. Some nights the troops got an issue of lime juice. Concerts were popular – 'the scenery made by black and red ink with curry powder for the green tints' – officers and men performing under the stars and regimental bands playing popular tunes. There was the Nile to bathe in and no ration on tea made with filtered water.

Sundays normally meant fresh bread, 'a welcome change from the eternal bully beef and biscuits' noted Lieutenant Meiklejohn of the Warwicks. Officers could send to England for a few luxuries such as soda water machines that helped improve their Scotch. Regimental messes tried to keep up appearances, even on a desert campaign; 'Had rather a fine breakfast,' noted Lieutenant Cox of the Lincolns just a few days after the Battle of the Atbara, 'kedgeree made of potted salmon and rice followed by bullock's heart and bacon!' Douglas Haig wrote home that the Egyptian Cavalry officers mess had meat, bread, bottled water and claret; he was 'really living in luxury.' For breakfast he ate Scotch porridge made with goat's milk, eggs, sausages and tinned bacon. Lunch consisted of soup, two meats, puddings with tinned fruit, while 'we have 6 champagne for tonight.'

The Royal Navy

The navy officered the ten gunboats Kitchener had at Omdurman. They were also crewed by civilian stokers and engineers, Royal Marine Artillery NCOs, native soldiers and crewmen. Three of the steamers – *Melik, Sheikh* and *Sultan* – were twin-screw steamers that had been specially built in Britain, shipped out in parts and reassembled in the Sudan. This work was done by a team under Major W. 'Monkey' Gordon, a nephew of the famous soldier.

14. The gunboat Melik *commanded by Major W. 'Monkey' Gordon RE during the battle.*

The Egyptian and Sudanese Troops

17,600 Egyptian and Sudanese troops fought at Omdurman, divided into 4 brigades along with 9 squadrons of Egyptian cavalry and 8 Camel Corps companies. Besides the 32nd and 37th Field Batteries, Royal Artillery, Colonel Long also commanded the 1st Egyptian Horse Battery and the 2nd, 3rd, 4th, 5th Egyptian Field Batteries.

Reformed after 1882, the senior officers of the Egyptian Army were all British, but several Arabs held important ranks; at Omdurman Fathy Bey commanded the 7th Egyptian Battalion in Lewis's Brigade, while Kiloussi Bey, who commanded the 8th Egyptian Battalion in the 2nd Brigade, had fought in the Russo-Turkish War.

Contracts were flexible and rates of pay and leave generous. Raw Egyptian conscripts had to serve six years with the colours and four with the reserve. Their pay was £E3.60 (Egyptian pounds) a year (plus rations) rising to £E18 for a warrant officer. The 9th–14th Battalions were Sudanese, formed mainly of blacks from the southern Sudan and Nuba mountains. Many had fought as dervishes in the original *jihadiyya* rifle corps before changing sides. They were well respected by their officers but conscripted for life.

The soldiers were well liked by their British comrades. In his diary on 31 July Private Teigh wrote: 'Three battalions of the Soudanese passed our camp for the front and we all turned out and gave them a good and hearty cheer for we knew they were good men, for they fought side by side with us at Atbara.' The 9th Sudanese were linked with the Cameron Highlanders after they fought side by side at Ginnis and were presented with a set of bagpipes. The 10th Sudanese treated the Lincolnshire boys to tea after their march from Berber.

Despite stinging insects, the fierce sun, hot desert sands and constant marching, the ordinary soldiers never lost their sense of humour. When, shortly before the big battle, a very tall Grenadier Guards officer asked a Warwickshire private if he had seen his company the man replied, 'I expect, Sir, they have got lost in the long grass.' Less witty but very typical was a remark overheard from one of the British NCOs in an Egyptian or Sudanese regiment as his men toiled to get a steamer through one of the Nile cataracts: 'Eave, yer buggers 'eave till I can cut weddin' rings off yer assholes!'

The Ansar

The intelligence expert Reginald Wingate estimated that the Mahdist army at Omdurman comprised 51,427 men, as stated in his Intelligence Report from Cairo, dated January 1899. However, the figure is highly suspect and open to revision, as he based it on old garrison returns found in the town after the battle, which seem to have been several years out of date (and explains such a specific figure). Participants in the battle have left conflicting accounts of the numbers. A study of lowest and highest figures in as many sources as I could find, and taking into account other factors – such as the fact that Shaykh al-Din's private guard of

2000 men sat out the fight though they are included in Wingate's very precise figure – gives a total of 40,350 dervishes on the battlefield. It seems possible that the final tally was around 45,000 men and certainly less than 51,000. We will never know for sure.

The ansar at Omdurman comprised warriors from all parts of the Sudan; frizzy haired Beja warriors from the Red Sea littoral mixed with the expert Baggara horsemen from sweltering Kordofan who formed the Khalifa's bodyguard, while black Africans from the south, west and Nuba mountains were recruited for the *mulazimiyya* rifle corps. In general terms the Black Flag drew warriors from the west of the country, the Green Flag recruited from the Dighaym, Kianan and al-Lahiwiyin Arabs of the region between the White and Blue Niles, while the river tribes and the Mahdi's own Danaqla flocked to the Red Flag.

Every 25 men were commanded by a *Muqaddem*, every 100 under a *Ra's Mia*, the units being grouped around the standard of an emir who, in turn, was subservient to a major flag. The basic tactical unit was the *Rub*; these could be several hundred to a few thousand warriors and were divided into spearmen, riflemen, cavalry and an administrative unit. In the 1890s the *mulazimiyya*, numbering 10–12,000 men armed with the best rifles, along with the Black Flag warriors, became the core of the dervish army.

The Mahdist state under the Khalifa was generally subject to sharia law but the army had its own code of military conduct; absence from camp or entering a city without permission were punishable by flogging. Senior emirs convicted of some offence would either be dismissed from the army or sent to Omdurman where the Khalifa could keep his eye on them.

The dervishes had been in action more or less continuously for almost two decades and each experienced warrior was now what Kipling rightly called 'a first-class fighting man'. It had taken the British some time to realise this fact, but by 1898 it was understood that the dervishes had the ability to break into the essential British fighting unit in a desert campaign, the packed square of infantry surrounding a headquarters corps, transport and supply. This had happened at Tamaii, Abu Klea and Tofrek. They had sprung any number of surprise attacks over the years and were utterly ferocious in close-quarter fighting. It rather unnerved the British that these simple men were so willing to die for their God, for if the sands of the Sudan was stained with English blood it had been drenched with that of thousands of dervishes. Up to a point there was a nationalist element, alongside a religious one, in all of this; many dervishes simply wanted foreigners, represented so long by the hated Egyptians, called 'Turks', to get out of their land. They knew that the rule of the Khalifa was not perfect but he was at least one of them. Others wanted a perfect world in the name of Allah; to die for the faith during a jihad was to be blessed.

On the day of the battle several 'volunteers' were encouraged to fight with the ansar. One of these, a student called Babikr Bedri, was drafted to the Black Flag. In his memoirs he confessed that after taking part in the initial attack and witnessing the firepower of the Sirdar's army, he smeared his face in a wounded man's blood and helped the fellow off the battlefield. For every three fanatical ansar who died that day, for every four who were wounded, there was probably another man simply trying to survive like Bedri.

The Kit

British Army

This consisted of regulation khaki uniform worn by all ranks with brown belts and white ammunition pouches. Buckles had to be sanded down. The khaki helmets had quilted neck curtains and officers got a new-style helmet with a flatter brim called 'the Wolseley'. Regiments marching through the dusty desert were distinguishable by a cotton patch and regimental badge worn on the helmet covers. The Lancashire Fusiliers, for example, had a square yellow patch, while the Grenadier Guards sported a blue and white rosette. The Rifle Brigade, who came late to the campaign, were provided with blue sun veils and goggles.

The 21st Lancers wore the same regulation uniform as the infantry, but with Bedford cord breeches of a fawn colour, and an MI bandolier instead of pouch belts. G.W. Steevens said the cavalry 'looked less like horsemen than Christmas trees', due to canteen-straps, carbines, haversacks, cloaks, swords, water bottles and other equipment they had to carry. Even the 21st Lancers referred to themselves as being 'in Christmas tree order'. Boots were a major cause for complaint in the Sudan and questions were asked in Parliament about the suitability of those supplied for desert conditions. General Gatacre did not endear himself to his men by ordering a forced march to Berber on four nights in full kit with minimal rations. 'What made the marching worse was that most of it was done in our bare feet,' recollected Private D. MacDonald of the Cameron Highlanders, 'as we had no shoes or sox [sic] on.'

British infantrymen were armed with the Lee Metford five-bullet magazine .303 calibre rifle firing a high velocity smokeless cordite bullet that had greater firepower than the Martini-Henry. It was completed by a 12-inch bayonet. The Lee Metford bullet, with its pencil diameter, was capable of drilling a hole through bone, but a rumour started that due to its nickel plating it would not stop a ferocious dervish. It was for this reason that Gatacre ordered his men to file down the tips of their bullets at the pointed end. This created dum-dums that the troops called 'man-stoppers', the effect being to make the bullet expand on impact, like an umbrella, leaving a gaping exit wound. Even so, in action the roughly cut dum-dums lost much of their accuracy in flight and jammed the rifle magazines when hot.

Cavalry were armed with the 1890 pattern sword. This was an unwieldy weapon that was unpopular throughout the decade. The 21st Lancers had been a hussar regiment until 1 April 1897; their new weapon was a nine-foot long bamboo lance weighing about five pounds with a hand-sling tied to the shaft at the armpit. Each weapon could be individually adjusted to suit the rider. The butt normally sat in a leather bucket fixed to the stirrup iron.

600 ROUNDS PER MINUTE

Sir Hiram Stevens Maxim (1840–1916), inventor of the famous machine gun, also claimed to be the originator of the common mouse trap! He certainly took out one of the first patents in the 1890s. His water-cooled gun, using the energy of the recoil to eject each spent cartridge and insert the next one, was a vast improvement on the hand-cranked Gatling, Gardner and Nordenfeldt guns. A prototype was taken on the Emin Pasha Relief Expedition 1886–90, but the weapon became famous after its use in the Matabele War of 1893.

British Horse and Field Artillery used 12-pounder and 15-pounder breech-loaders with a light carriage, firing a new shell with high fragmentation. 5.5-inch howitzers fired lyddite – a new explosive adopted for its bursting charge – that tore holes in the dome of the Mahdi's tomb during the battle. The most deadly weapon in the Sirdar's arsenal was the Maxim gun; it weighed less than 40lbs, its barrel could be fully traversed from side to side and it was capable of firing ten rounds a second accurate up to 2500 yards.

Egyptian and Sudanese Troops

The Egyptians wore a khaki tunic and trousers, blue puttees, a red fez with khaki cover and a neck cloth, while the Sudanese had plaited straw fez covers. Beneath their jackets the Egyptians wore brown jerseys and the Sudanese dark blue. Each battalion was recognisable by the specific flash on its fez covers. On campaign each battalion carried a plain green silk battle standard bearing its number in white Arabic numerals. Each company also carried a small cloth on a shaft of some kind with its number at the centre.

The Egyptian Army used the black powder Martini-Henry rifle with its infamous vicious recoil on the shoulder but considerable stopping power. It was equipped with the 1886–87 new pattern

18.5-inch bayonet – a weapon in itself at close quarters! Both Egyptian and British troops made use of trigger-fired Maxim guns, cooled by a water jacket and cartridges in a flexible belt, but only the Egyptian cavalry had a 'galloping Maxim battery' drawn by a team of six horses.

Mahdist Troops

The Mahdist kit made the soldiers an instantly recognisable fighting force; after the capture of El Obeid in 1883 the Mahdi had declared that his ansar should wear only a white cotton smock with coloured patches known as a *jibbah*, white trousers, sandals, a girdle of plaited straw, a white skull cap and beads. The turban was wrapped around the skull cap 'in a distinctive way, which was in itself a badge of Mahdiism'. Some carried a *rukwa*, or leather pot, for ritual ablutions. Richer dervishes might even take a slave

15. A contemporary photograph of an unknown dervish emir, clearly posed, but accurate in garb and weapons.

to carry their *rukwa* and utensils for food and making tea. The emirs and sheikhs also carried a death shroud folded in the shape of a bag. This proved they were ready to die on the battlefield. A few sheikhs also rode into battle like crusader knights, wearing chainmail vests and waving their cross-hilted swords.

Flags and battle standards were carried into battle; the Black Flag, for instance, was six feet square atop a 20-foot pole. Ansar rallied to the battle standards of their different commanders and sub-commanders. These colourful flags were about four feet by three feet, usually bordered in white, with texts from the Koran and Allah's name picked out in green letters.

From their early battles the dervishes had amassed a large arsenal of weapons; they had about 15,000 rifles at Omdurman, mainly American Remingtons, capable of firing 17 rounds a minute. Unfortunately, dervish fire was always weak since, in the excitement of the fight, they usually fired too high. Many Mahdists shortened their barrels with the usual disastrous results. Captured or homemade bandoliers were strung about the waist. The dervishes fired their weapons from the waist as they stood or even ran; to lie down and take careful aim was tantamount to cowardice.

The majority of infantrymen carried a ten-foot broad-bladed thrusting spear, plus three shorter throwing spears and a long double-edged sword. These cross-hilted, medieval looking swords were cheaply made using scrap metal from discarded rail tracks. Short daggers were strapped to the upper arm under the jibbah, and protection came in the form of a small round shield with a conical boss, made of tough crocodile, elephant or rhinoceros hide, though shields were normally frowned upon by most dervishes, except the eastern Sudan Beja tribes.

One of the ansar's main weaknesses was their failure to exploit the heavy guns in the Omdurman arsenal and held in the mud forts by the Nile: 35 brass mountain guns, 8 Krupp cannon, 7 machine guns and 13 others including some acquired in Abyssinia. Two of the Khalifa's three river steamers also had a mountain gun apiece. In the final battle Osman Azrak used some cannon and five guns were placed on a hill and fired near the Black Flag troops, but they were remarkably ineffective; more than 40 rounds were fired during the battle and an eyewitness declared that 'the fuses were beautifully timed and the projectiles burst at an excellent height above the ground', but the range was too long and in general they never reached their targets.

The reason for this failure to exploit heavy artillery lay in the dervish belief that its primary function was to bombard fortifications, not to be used against an army. Abdullahi also knew that his locally manufactured gunpowder was so weak that the explosive charge could not propel a shell very far; cases were made from Sudanese-mined light copper or brass. At the Battle of the Atbara, for example, Piper Mackenzie of the Seaforths was shot six times but was not injured, the weak powder just leaving scorch marks on his tunic. The Mahdist shells made a loud explosion but did not burst out shrapnel fragments. The actual Mahdist gunners, it is worth adding, were former Egyptian soldiers captured in battle and it appears that they were not too keen to assist the dervishes by firing on their own countrymen.

Supply and Transport

The 1896–98 re-conquest of the Sudan is a study in logistics; Kitchener was told to conduct his campaign with a careful regard to costs. Each step on the road to Omdurman was thought out by him prudently and economically; he intended to avoid the mistakes made by the Gordon Relief Expedition. Kitchener knew he was no tactician, but he *was* a Royal Engineer, and he planned the advance to Omdurman with an engineer's outlook. Supply and transport were supremely important and in this respect the campaign was a masterpiece.

Just to get his troops from Cairo to the Sudan frontier required travelling 350 miles by railway to Balliana, transferring for the next 30 miles to Aswan on a fleet of Messrs Thos. Cook's travel company Nile steamers (with the baggage on a fleet of Nile barges

16. The flotilla – the Nile advance was necessarily slow yet painstakingly planned by Kitchener.

and native sailing boats), then rejoining a railway for 6 miles to skirt around the First Cataract, then the river again for 208 miles to Wadi Halfa, and a further 33 miles to Saras in the Sudan on an old narrow-gauge railway left over from the 1884–85 expedition.

Kitchener's 'Band of Boys' – young Royal Engineer officers under the command of a 29-year-old monocled French-Canadian, Lieutenant Edouard Girouard – designed and ran the Sudan Military Railway, built with native labour. It started just across the frontier at Saras and, under Girouard and the Sirdar's watchful eyes, crept forward steadily at one and a half miles a day. Repair and other workshops followed along the line as these railway pioneers grew increasingly expert at driving their track across inhospitable desert terrain.

Animal transport received the same careful scrutiny. Kitchener's brother, Walter, a major in the West Yorkshires who had been a transport officer in the Second Afghan War, was brought from India to take charge of the camels. Two thousand of these beasts, some even fitted with sun bonnets and loaded with supplies, toiled up the Nile.

In contrast the dervishes, like most native armies, lived mainly off the land while on campaign. Women and children often followed in their wake, emirs took their servants, the whole mass travelling in a vast cloud of dust. The army could request supplies of grain from the various garrisons scattered about the country. The Nile was utilised, with steamers, barges and rafts ferrying supplies such as ammunition, which was not usually entrusted to camels. Officials of the Omdurman treasury were responsible for provisioning the army.

Tactics

The Sirdar's battle plan will be dealt with in detail later on, so here we restrict ourselves to the general observation that what Kitchener intended was to get his army safely up the Nile and bring the dervishes to battle near the river, or on a plain, where he could unleash his massive firepower: from infantry rifles, heavy artillery and machine guns in the desert as well as his flotilla on the Nile. Kitchener was well aware of the damage that could be done to his troops if the dervishes got to close quarters; the enemy had to be wiped out at a distance. He knew that a dervish night attack on the eve of the battle could be disastrous but in the event they missed this opportunity. He was also lucky that the Khalifa did not plan a defence of Omdurman itself, where the British could have taken heavy losses in street-to-street fighting.

Kitchener's basic plan was to get to Omdurman by stages as his forward troops were supplied after each careful advance by camel convoys until the Sudan Railway was sufficiently built to pour in men and supplies. The rising summer Nile would allow him to get gunboats (assembled in sections) and supply ships past the cataracts.

Traditionally the Mahdists had developed a technique of shock and surprise. This was used towards the end of the Battle of Omdurman and might have succeeded but the wide plain, with little cover, was not the best place for this kind of attack. The master of this kind of warfare was Osman Digna, who used to position his men behind rocks or in thorny scrub where they would lie undetected before springing up to attack. Massed attacks took on a wedge formation as the bravest and strongest raced forwards fastest. Once they penetrated an enemy's defence line the breach was automatically widened by warriors pouring in from behind. The Beja were particularly adept at cutting the ligaments of camels with their curved knives, bringing down their riders or supplies. In a close quarters attack the same tribesmen, like the famously fuzzy-haired Hadendowa, would sometimes slash at a British soldier's ankles and bring him to the ground where he could be quickly disembowelled.

Such effective and vicious fighting did not take place at Omdurman. Abdullahi's generalship was appalling; having thrown away a night attack on Kitchener's zariba prior to the battle, against the advice of his best generals, he then launched two armies apiece at Omdurman in two phases. For the Mahdists, everything depended on timing and the enemy's response. The plan was flexible but, as one expert has noted, 'The main flaw was his [the Khalifa's] complete ignorance of the enemy – in contrast to the enemy's knowledge of his forces and dispositions.'

THE RE-CONQUEST BEGINS

Why It Happened

When the news came it caught everyone unawares. From Cairo in late February 1896 Baring (raised to the peerage as Lord Cromer), had been asking if it might be possible to stage a ' military diversion' to help take pressure off the Italians who were fighting the dervishes in their small colony of Eritrea on the Red Sea coast, south of Suakin. Lord Salisbury refused, saying on 29 February, that 'The power of the Khalifa tends steadily to diminish and a waiting game is the obvious policy.' Next day an Italian army of 18,000 men, planning to conquer Abyssinia, were wiped out by the very natives they despised. It was the worst European loss of arms ever encountered in Africa and it left the Italians utterly humiliated. On 10 March the Italian ambassador in London told Lord Salisbury that Abyssinians and Mahdist armies were advancing on Eritrea and begged for a British show of force to ease the strain. Salisbury and his Cabinet now saw the usefulness of helping the Italians and preventing the dervishes from 'winning a conspicuous success which might have far-reaching results'. An advance towards Dongola, capital of the Sudan's northern province, was sanctioned.

There was a deeper motive; as Salisbury explained to Cromer: 'We desired to kill two birds with one stone, and to use the same military effort to plant the foot of Egypt rather further up the Nile.' With the European powers scrambling for African colonies, the British had set their sights on control of the Nile valley from as far away as Uganda. Other countries needed to be kept out, especially the French, who, it was rumoured, were secretly planning to approach the Upper Nile from West Africa and plant their flag. For this reason Salisbury had not wanted to expend men and money in the backwaters of the Eastern Sudan at Suakin, 'because there would be no ulterior profit in these movements' such as those the Nile afforded. Privately, Salisbury wished 'our Italian friends had less capacity for being beaten, but it would not have been safe from an African or European point of view to sit quite still while they were being crushed.' To keep the Queen happy he told her Khartoum was 'the ultimate object', but the Cabinet were agreed 'We must see how things go.'

Caution was the byword of the whole enterprise. Cromer accepted that 'We want (1) to get sooner or later to Dongola (2) to resist the almost inevitable pressure to go further than Dongola.' He knew that 'eventually Khartoum will have to be recovered', but advised 'a very long halt at Dongola – perhaps two or three years', before a final advance. Cromer would be the pivot, controlling Kitchener, while in turn the Foreign Office would control the campaign, neatly bypassing the War Office in London. It also helped that one of the Prime Minister's sons, Lord Edward Cecil of the Grenadier Guards, would be on the Sirdar's staff so 'All shall be known at home by the proper people.'

The Initial Egyptian Advance

Salisbury's telegram reached Kitchener in the early hours of 13 March. So delighted was he by the news that he danced a jig in his pyjamas, which must have been a rare sight indeed! Three days later, while Cromer was still making his financial plans and telling the Khedive to ignore the Ottoman sultan's veto on the use of the Egyptian Army, those same troops moved across the Sudan

17. Egyptian infantry advance on the Mahdists at Firka, 7 June 1896.

frontier; 87 miles over the border they reached the dervish village of Akasha, found it deserted, and occupied it. Sixteen miles away, across the black rocky hills known as the 'Belly of Stones', lay a dervish outpost at Firka. Its commander was warned by the dervish governor of Dongola, Wad Bishara, to be 'quite prepared and on the watch, as I have received information that the God-forsaken Sirdar says that he will occupy the district in seven weeks.'

Firka was a jumble of mud huts stretching for nearly a mile along the east bank of the Nile. Wad Bishara demoted its commander, the Emir Hammuda, with a veteran campaigner, Osman Azrak. In a plan devised by Archibald Hunter and approved by Kitchener the attacking force would be divided into two columns called 'River' and 'Desert'. Hunter would lead the River Column consisting of the 1st (Lewis's), 2nd (MacDonald's) and 3rd (Maxwell's) infantry brigades with two field batteries – a compliment of about 7000 men. The Desert Column, under the cavalry commander Miralai Burn-Murdoch, included seven squadrons of cavalry, eight Camel Corps companies, a horse artillery battery and the Maxim machine guns of the North Staffords and Connaughts – the only British troops involved – plus an extra battalion of Sudanese from

18. A group of dervishes taken prisoner during the Firka battle. Men like these often joined the Egyptian Army.

MacDonald's brigade who were mounted on camels. These 2000 desert troops would march away from the river and outflank the dervishes on the nearby hills before coming up to menace the enemy's rear.

The dawn attack on 7 June went off like clockwork. More than 800 dervishes were killed – many in house-to-house fighting – and 600 were taken prisoner. The Egyptian Army lost just 20 men killed and 83 wounded. Osman Azrak escaped but the Emir Hammuda died on the battlefield. Firka was acclaimed a great success, especially by the newspapers, but Hunter felt his troops shot badly: 'The IX were too quick if anything. The XI couldn't keep up – The III distinguished itself – steady as a rock, good volleys, no cursing, a grim silence … The 3rd Bn III Bde practically did nothing.'

On to Hafir and Dongola

The next eight weeks saw the troops facing a new enemy –
cholera. Hospital facilities were primitive in the sweltering desert
and almost 1000 soldiers and camp followers died. Despite these
setbacks, with the Nile at its highest in August, four gunboats

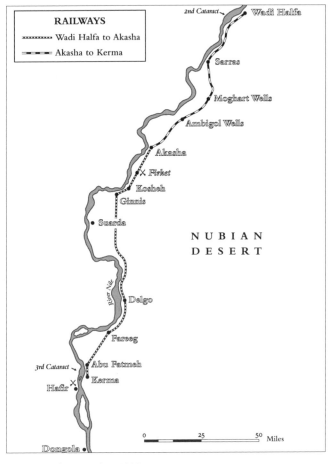

The Dongola Campaign, 1896.

and three transport steamers were somehow got over the Second Cataract by tugging teams of sweating soldiers, local natives and convicts, the latter 'encouraged' by the lash.

Work on the railway also never stopped. In August freak dust storms swept away a large section of embankment. The Sirdar took personal charge of the repair work as 35,000 men laboured in the blistering sun to complete the job.

A brains team had evolved; combined with the wonderful transport planning of Girouard and his Royal Engineer colleagues, Kitchener had the efficient Hunter commanding his fighting men and Wingate's vigilant intelligence service. With slender financial resources this remarkable linguist had created a subtle system perfect in every detail. 'His secret service honeycombed the Sudan,' wrote Kitchener's official biographer, 'and in the guise of merchants, holy men, artisans, wandering beggars, and even women, his spies penetrated the fastnesses of Dervishdom and brought back information acquired at first hand.' Around him Wingate gathered a small yet skilful team of interrogators and analysts. His right-hand man was a Syrian Christian, Milhem Bey Shakoor, but his most famous aide was Rudolph von Slatin, who had been imprisoned by the Khalifa for twelve years before he escaped in 1895. With Wingate's help he wrote an account of his sufferings called *Fire and Sword in the Sudan*, a runaway bestseller in 1896 and a propaganda coup that popularised the war.

Once his delays were overcome, Kitchener was keen to push on with his 15,000-strong army. By 19 September they reached Kerma near Dongola. Kitchener had expected to find the place defended but overnight the wily Wad Bishara, displaying 'one of the few shrewd tactical moves made by a Mahdist commander in the campaign', has shipped his entire force to entrenched positions on the other side of the Nile at Hafir. Here Kitchener's three gunboats, *Tamaii, Abu Klea* and *Metemma* (a fourth, *El Teb*, was stuck on a rock at the Third Cataract), bringing with them the Egyptian troops reinforced by the North Staffordshire Regiment, ran into fairly accurate dervish fire. The battle developed into an

RAILWAY BUILDER EXTRAORDINAIRE

Edouard Percy Girouard was born in Montreal, Canada, in 1867. He entered the Canadian Royal Military College aged fifteen and soon showed outstanding promise as an engineer. Girouard decided to specialise in railway construction. Girouard, nicknamed 'Gerry', began work on the Sudan Military Railway at Wadi Halfa in March 1896. The task was huge – laying a track across the desert, bringing up supplies and men, training Egyptians as engineers and track-layers, combating the perils of nature, especially the heat, coping with inefficiency and human error. Added to all this, Kitchener told him, 'Don't spend too much Girouard. We are all terribly poor.' But the task was done with the help of a dedicated band of enthusiastic young Royal Engineer officers. Girouard went on to run the Sudan railways after the war and build others in South Africa.

19. Edouard Percy
Cranwell Girouard, the
French-Canadian railway
builder.

artillery duel between the Egyptian gunners on one side and the Mahdist riflemen on the other. That night the dervishes slipped away into the desert and it took Kitchener two days to get his army over to the west bank on which Dongola lay, 35 miles upsteam. Everyone was expecting a big battle. But approaching the town the Connaughts and North Staffords, perhaps the last British infantry ever to wear red on campaign, saw dervish cavalry disappearing into the desert. Thus, after a long trek, Dongola was captured in a bloodless anti-climax. Yet the Sirdar had, in just six months, recovered 450 miles of the Nile valley at the low cost of 47 officers and men killed in action and 122 wounded and an expenditure of only £E715,000.

Dongola to Abu Hamed

Immediately Dongola was taken Kitchener hurried back to Cairo and then on to London to press for a continuation of his campaign. In the streets of the capital he was cheered (the newspapers were full of his achievements, especially the jingoistic *Daily Mail* and *Daily Telegraph*), Queen Victoria made him a knight and a major-general. He was only 46 years old. The Prime Minister gave his approval for the war to continue as Kitchener was boarding his return train. In February 1897 the British government loaned

LITTLE DONKEY

The Sudan advance has developed delightful legends over the years; one concerns Lieutenant Graham Bowman-Manifold RE and his 65 donkeys. According to Winston Churchill a novel method of laying a desert telegraph was created by letting the spools of wire unwind off the donkeys' backs as they trotted along. In fact the wire drums had to be unloaded by hand and then unwound – a wearisome job. To save time and without transport no poles were used, and the little donkeys, trudging over the barren sands, remain unsung heroes.

Egypt £800,000 to defray war costs while the Chancellor of the Exchequer told Parliament 'Egypt could never be permanently secure so long as a hostile Power was in occupation of the Nile valley up to Khartoum.'

The die had, of course, been long cast and history was forged in the sand by the tracks and rivets of the Sudan Military Railway. Kitchener and Girouard next decided to build a line across the Nubian desert from Wadi Halfa to Abu Hamed, a distance of 230 miles. This would avoid striking for Khartoum across the vast Bayuda desert which had been such an obstacle to Wolseley's expedition in 1884. From Abu Hamed the railway could be extended on to Berber near the junction of the Nile and Atbara rivers. The first spike was struck on 1 January 1897. 'The speed of the advance was hindered by dust-storms, derailments, decrepit locomotives, inexperience of the subordinate staff, an engineering strike in England, lack of sleepers in Egypt … insufficiency of transport on the lower Nile and a dozen other causes.' Yet in ten months the job was done.

In July, when the railway was about halfway to Abu Hamed, the Sirdar ordered Hunter to put himself at the head of a flying column

20. Laying tracks for the Sudan Military Railway.

21. 'Pushing on to the front.' SMR work crews were self-contained with regards to supplies and equipment.

of 3600 troops, the cream of the army, and to surprise the enemy at Abu Hamed and cut off their retreat to Berber. He was told to construct a fort there but to proceed no further. Abu Hamed was a sizable town protected by three high watchtowers. Creeping forward at dawn on 7 August 1897 the Egyptians were spotted by an alert dervish lookout. Shots rang out as Hunter led his forces in a wide circuit of the town, then swung them in a right arc to face the enemy, his order of battle being, from his left, 10th and 9th Sudanese, 3rd Egyptian and 11th Sudanese, with his artillery in the centre. After about half an hour's bombardment he sent his troops forward. It was vicious bayonet work in the streets with no quarter asked or given; 450 dervishes were killed at a loss of just 18 Egyptians and Sudanese killed and 61 wounded.

The captured dervish commander defiantly told Hunter that the Mahdists would still 'wipe you out'. Hunter replied by tying some dead dervishes into small bundles and letting them float down the Nile so that the Sirdar could learn of his success.

The advance continued; the gunboat *El Teb* was wrecked at the Fourth Cataract but five others reached Abu Hamed by 29 August; the Camel Corps probed the Bayuda desert and Lord Cromer gave his permission for an advance on Berber. Lying 130

ROYAL BLOOD SPILLED

A great-grandson of King William IV died at the Battle of Abu Hamed. He was 32-year-old Bimbashi Edward Fitzclarence, 11th Sudanese, who, along with his commanding officer, Kaimakan Henry Sidney, were the only two British officers of the Egyptian Army killed in action during the 1896–99 Sudan re-conquest.

miles further up the Nile, it was hoped that its occupation would impress the river tribes and those to the east where allegiance to the Mahdist cause was faltering. To secure Berber, Hunter took an advance party of half a battalion of the 9th Sudanese in the four gunboats. He found it a ruined ghost town compared with twelve years earlier. A relieved Kitchener hurried there himself, bringing five battalions by 22 September.

The Sirdar was working himself towards a nervous breakdown: his staff was tiny but he refused to delegate (he told his Chief of Staff, Leslie Rundle, to 'stay quiet and not fuss'); Osman Digna was once again stirring up the tribes along the Red Sea littoral; former Sirdar Francis Grenfell had just been appointed C-in-C of the British Army of Occupation in Egypt and Kitchener feared he might be replaced by him; and there was a continual battle with the financial controllers in Cairo. In late October Kitchener handed in his resignation – then just as quickly withdrew it. A jittery Cromer told Lord Salisbury: 'Those who know Kitchener best tell me that he is liable to fits of extreme depression from which, however, he rapidly recovers … In the meantime his frame of mind causes me some anxiety, for everything depends on his keeping his head, and judging calmly of the situation.' The Sirdar, still outwardly reserved, confessed to a friend,

I hope there will be no question about finishing the whole thing off at Omdurman next year. The strain on all of us, and the troops, is very great, and if we do not continue the advance, the dervishes will certainly resume the offensive … I do not think that I can stand much more, and I feel so done up that I can hardly go on and wish I were dead.

The man G.W. Steevens described as a machine was, in fact, human.

Once the railway got to Abu Hamed the engineers only had 17 miles of unused track laying material, so a further advance would have to wait a few weeks. Then Reginald Wingate got news that the Khalifa was sending large reinforcements to his emir, Mahmud, and it was clear a large battle could be expected. It was time for Kitchener to get everything in place for the final push on Omdurman. To do this he needed more troops and they would have to arrive, acclimatise and fight a battle fairly soon on the Atbara. A request for British troops was sent on New Year's Day 1898.

ATBARA TO EVE
OF BATTLE

British Troops Arrive

By late February 1898 a British Infantry Brigade under Major-General Gatacre had slogged to Berber; it consisted of the 1st battalions of the Warwicks, Lincolns and Cameron Highlanders (all part of the British Army of Occupation in Egypt), supported by Royal Artillery (including six Maxim guns), and a company of Royal Engineers. Fresh from Malta, the 1st Battalion of the Seaforth Highlanders joined the brigade after a short spell in Egypt.

Perhaps to prove himself a fighting commander and impress Kitchener, Gatacre led his men on the last leg to Berber by a forced march across the desert. The troops set off on 26 February and arrived on the morning of 3 March. It was so tough that some men fell asleep marching, others had no skin on their feet and several fell out with sunstroke. Egyptian bands played them into Berber and regiments lined up to cheer. Lieutenant Cox of the Lincolns had seven blisters on his feet and felt the men's confidence in Gatacre was shaken – 'He has the reputation of wearing out his troops unnecessarily.'

During December 1897 and January 1898 the great war drum had boomed out across Omdurman and councils were held late into the night. The Khalifa Abdullahi talked of jihad, spurred on by the likelihood that the opportunistic Abyssinians might send an army to support him. It was all a dream; they just wanted time to re-occupy some border territory. Abdullahi was also vexed by harsh words between his brother Ya'qub and eldest son, Shaykh al-Din. Then, on 27 January, the drumming stopped; Abdullahi had decided not to march an army down the Nile but to await the Anglo-Egyptians at Omdurman.

The Emir Mahmud wad Ahmed – the Khalifa's principal commander in the north (and also his nephew) – had repressed a revolt at Metemma in 1897 massacring over 2000 of its inhabitants. Missing an opportunity to fortify Berber and hold onto it ahead of the Sirdar's troops, trying to keep together a discontented army, he awaited instructions from the Khalifa. The word finally came advising a withdrawal to Omdurman. Mahmud refused; he felt it would have a harmful effect on morale and lead to further desertions. For weeks he had been begging for reinforcements; these now arrived under Osman Digna who brought 4000 ansar. But the extra numbers only added to Mahmud's problems and it left the warriors with a divided command.

The 14,000-strong Anglo-Egyptian Army was now on the Atbara and so in early February the dervishes started to move out to meet them. Soon the two emirs were quarrelling; Mahmud wanted to stick close to the Nile, but Osman Digna pointed out that this left the ansar at the mercy of Kitchener's gunboats. Reaching Nakheila on the Atbara, the Emir Mahmud decided to build a defensive thorn *zariba* amid a grove of dom trees. Osman Digna was aghast; he pointed out that the position on low ground was vulnerable and any camp near the main Nile and Atbara rivers made it easy for the Sirdar to launch a dawn attack after a night's march. He advised that they draw the enemy further into the desert, away from his river support, realising that the Sirdar would have no option but to follow and force a battle, unless he was willing to leave his flank and lines of communication open to dervish attacks. The Khalifa approved Osman's plan but Mahmud refused to listen. He wanted a fight.

The military critic General Sir Frederick Maxse argued that the fault lay with the Khalifa who failed to reinforce Mahmud. If he had done so then he undoubtedly would have attacked the Anglo-Egyptian lines of communication sooner, and 'it is doubtful whether Kitchener could have maintained his position if a substantial Dervish body had threatened him.' Yet despite errors on the parts of Abdullahi and Mahmud, and despite a gap between the opposing forces of just 20 miles, Kitchener still did not know the exact position of the 12,000-strong ansar. The task of locating it fell to Broadwood and his 800 Egyptian cavalry troopers. Mahmud was supposed to have upwards of 3000 horsemen so a fortnight of vicious and incessant reconnaissance began.

It was bad country for cavalry – stony desert fissured by dry water courses called *khors*. After ten days of scouting the main dervish camp had still not been sighted and so Broadwood, with Hunter riding along in a non-executive role, was ordered to lead a decisive patrol on 5 April. A deserter from Mahmud's army led the eight cavalry squadrons, one battery of horse artillery, four galloping Maxims and an infantry brigade directly to the dervish zariba. Hunter (with field glasses) got within 300 yards before he even realised what it was. Despite a flurry of activity from their guns and Maxims the Egyptian troops quickly withdrew. Quicker off the mark were the dervish cavalry who used the cover of a dust cloud to get close during the retreat and total Egyptian losses were 10 men and horses killed and 16 men and 19 horses wounded. 'At one time it looked uncommonly as if they would bag the lot of us,' recollected Miralai John Maxwell, 'We were completely surrounded by their horsemen and could not see a yard for dust, bullets fizzing about, and had a real attack been pushed home, they would undoubtedly have got the lot of us, as we were too far in the desert for any of us to have got away.' Another participant, referring to the Second Afghan War disaster, called it, 'Maiwand again, only properly done.'

Waiting, wondering, full of uncertainty, Kitchener decided next day to hold a council of war with Hunter, Wingate and Gatacre.

Perhaps made nervous by what had happened to the cavalry, Hunter for once advised against an attack, while Gatacre and the others urged Kitchener to fight. Knowing that tactics were his weakness, a 'perplexed' Sirdar asked Cromer what he should do. This message was relayed to Whitehall and Salisbury showed the telegram to Lord Wolseley, now Commander-in-Chief, at the War Office. He replied, 'You have a first-rate man in command. Trust him and let him do as he thinks best.' (Later the Field-Marshal privately scolded Kitchener, saying: 'Were I in your place, I would not, however, ask such a question.') Cromer wired caution but before his telegram arrived Hunter had been won over; they would attack on 8 April – Good Friday.

The Battle of the Atbara

Approaching Mahmud's zariba from the desert, with the dry bed of the Atbara behind it, the Anglo-Egyptian infantry formed a curved line running approximately 1500 yards. They would make an old-style bayonet charge with the British Brigade (from left facing the zariba), the 2nd and 1st Egyptian Brigades (the 3rd held in reserve). Two batteries of artillery supported each brigade and there was a rocket battery commanded by Lieutenant David Beatty RN. Further out in the desert, left of the line, were the cavalry and galloping Maxims.

The Sirdar's order to his army, handed out on 7 April, ended with the words, 'Remember Gordon. The men before you are murderers.' The Anglo-Egyptians approached the zariba through the night, infantry marching and resting in brigade squares, arriving at dawn to form up some 800 yards away. At 6.15am the artillery opened fire and kept up a barrage for 90 minutes. Dom trees, bushes and straw huts caught fire but nothing seemed to stir in the dervish camp as they lay in their trenches and waited for the explosions to end.

It was the most glorious day in Major-General Gatacre's life and he was determined to relish every second of it; standing at the

22. A stylised illustration of the Battle of the Atbara which gives some idea of its fierceness.

head of the British troops, a Union flag held by Lance-Sergeant Wyeth of the Army Service Corps, he drew out his sword and prepared to charge on foot at the head of his men. Bugles sounded the advance and accompanied by drummers drumming and bagpipes wailing, the long line of British infantry marched forward 'as slow as a funeral'. Soldiers watched in awe as a huge flock of vultures on their left rose into the morning air. Not so the Egyptians who surged ahead with Maxwell's Brigade slightly ahead of MacDonald's. These two commanders, along with Hunter, rode into battle.

The silence seemed ominous to Lieutenant Meiklejohn of the Warwicks: 'Then we moved up a gentle rise, at the top of which we found ourselves looking down on the zariba some 300 yards from us. Still no sound.' Gatacre allowed his men a few seconds rest as they fired a volley. This was met, at last, by a return volley from Mahmud's riflemen. Thousands of bullets whizzed slightly overhead of the troops. Lieutenant Cox, leading some of the Lincolns, took a bullet through his helmet just as a sergeant got hit mortally in the mouth. The fire grew intense; Private Southall, with Meiklejohn, was badly wounded in the shoulder but saluted with his hand and asked that he might fall out. Men fell everywhere as the Egyptian advance was reduced to a series of short spurts. The artillery had recommenced firing and the noise of shell fire, rifles and Maxims bludgeoned the senses.

Reaching the zariba Meiklejohn thought it 'a miserable affair', just branches of tangled thornbush about four feet high and a few feet thick. With sword in his right hand and revolver in the left he took a running jump at it and fell sprawling inside, while Captain Findlay of the Camerons was shot dead close by. Some men used their blankets wrapped around hands to push back the thorns. A dervish charged at Gatacre who, totally unfazed, told his orderly, 'Give him the bayonet, lad.' The flag-waving Wyeth had been mortally wounded so Gatacre's ADC was pressed into service to hold the Union standard high as the general strode purposefully into the dervish camp.

23. One of the trenches in the Mahdist zariba at the Atbara filled with dead.

Inside it was hell; Lieutenant Manifold RE described it as 'pits full of hobbled donkeys, alive, dead and wounded; camels knocked inside out; dead and wounded men with burning garments; dead and wounded women, often naked, and shattered by shot and shell.' 'The blacks went through the zariba like paper,' wrote Walter Kitchener; even dervishes offering the traditional mimosa sprig of submission, or holding up their hands, were shot and bayoneted. The British Brigade loosed off about 23,000 rounds inside the zariba and the Egyptian Brigade in excess of 100,000 rounds, both indicators of the savagery of the fight. Lieutenant Meiklejohn heard a voice shout out, 'Now you're into them Warwickshire lads. Stick every mother's son!' The British officers were generally appalled at the gusto with which their men seemed to spare nothing except the animals. 'The smell was a bit like a slaughter house,' recalled Cox. When a dervish dropped his weapon and begged for mercy a Cameron Highlanders sergeant told a private, 'We don't want none of these buggers 'ere' and the poor man was bayoneted twice. Dervishes fleeing to the Atbara were shot down in their hundreds until the stagnant pools turned blood red, while inside the zariba, 'there was a horrible smell of roasting flesh.'

Bugles sounded assembly. It had taken just 45 minutes from the initial advance. Kitchener now rode through the camp to tumultuous cheers. He looked and, indeed was, deeply affected since he had worried much before the battle and determined, if he lost, never to return to England again.

The Egyptian and Sudanese wounded were quickly looked after but medical care for the British was slow to arrive (to Kitchener's fury). The final butcher's bill was estimated to be 81 officers and men killed and 478 wounded. Around the zariba, along the dry river bed and in the sieve of trenches lay over 3000 Mahdist warriors, the Emir Wad Bishara amongst them, while another 4000 were taken prisoner, 'poor wretches, many had terrible wounds', recalled Douglas Haig.

The Emir Mahmud was found hiding beneath a bed in a pit of his headquarters area of the camp. He was defiant and limped with

24. Proud and defiant, the handsome Emir Mahmud taken prisoner at the Atbara. The bloodstains are those of one of his bodyguard killed during the fight.

a small bayonet wound to the leg. His jibbah was wet with blood (though Mahmud later explained that it was not his but that of an aide who died protecting him). British officers were impressed to find he was an extremely handsome Sudanese black of about 30 years, shaven-headed, with a good physique and a proud attitude. The Sirdar asked him in Arabic why he 'come into my country to burn and kill?' 'Same as you,' replied a defiant Mahmud, 'I have to obey the Khalifa's orders as you must the Khedive's.' He was asked several questions and admitted Osman Digna had left, adding, 'I am not a woman to run away.' The young emir let fly a last retort as he was marched into captivity: 'You will pay for all this at Omdurman. Compared with the Khalifa I am but a leaf.'

Final Preparations

A less wary commander than Kitchener might have gambled on a dash towards Omdurman. But the Sirdar was not that kind of a man; after the cheers had died down and the troops recovered from the savage slaughter he put his army into summer quarters between Fort Atbara and Berber while steadily accumulating supplies, increasing his naval arsenal and watching the Nile rise. Early in June he left the front for Cairo and then slipped away quickly to London for a few days. Several of his officers also took some leave.

During July and August a 2nd British Brigade was formed consisting of the 1st Battalion Grenadier Guards from Gibraltar, the 1st Battalion Northumberland Fusiliers and 2nd Battalion Lancashire Fusiliers from Cairo and the 2nd Battalion Rifle Brigade from Malta. Hunter's Egyptian troops were reinforced by a 4th Egyptian Brigade, the Camel Corps was expanded from six to eight companies and Broadwood got an additional cavalry squadron to complement the existing eight. Extra artillery in the shape of the 32nd and 37th Field Batteries of Royal Artillery armed with 5-inch howitzers and 9-pounders arrived along with a Royal Irish Fusiliers Maxim battery with four mule-drawn machine guns.

The most notable new arrivals, on 15 August, were a single regiment of British cavalry, the 21st Lancers. Despite wags who satirically sniffed that the regiment's total lack of battle honours suggested its motto ought to be 'Thou shalt not kill', its second-in-command, Major W. Crole-Wyndham, along with Major J. Fowle commanding 'B' squadron, had both served in the 1884–85 Sudan Expedition, while Major H. Finn of 'A' squadron had won a DCM fighting in Afghanistan with another cavalry regiment.

Soon to be more famous than any of these gallant soldiers was a 23-year-old subaltern who had snuk into the regiment in the hope of seeing active service. His name was Winston Leonard Spencer Churchill. Ambitious and pushy, Churchill had made several attempts to join the Sirdar's army. Each one was bluntly snubbed by Kitchener who considered him an aristocratic upstart with little useful military experience. He would have been even more livid had he realised that Churchill intended also to act as a war correspondent for *The Morning Post* at £15 an article. Churchill, for his part, wrote privately that Kitchener 'may be a

Winston S. Churchill
Sept. 2. 1898

25. The young cavalryman Winston Churchill in his campaign dress.

general – but never a gentleman.' The young officer luckily had a champion in Sir Evelyn Wood, now Adjutant-General at the War Office in London, who under pressure from Churchill's beautiful and redoubtable mother Jennie and others, agreed that it was not Kitchener's job to staff or veto officers in the British units. In the third week of July Lieutenant Churchill of the 4th Hussars, got the following missive:

> You have been attached as a supernumerary Lieutenant to the 21st Lancers for the Soudan Campaign. You are to report at once at the Abassiyeh Barracks, Cairo, to the Regimental Headquarters. It is understood that you will proceed at your own expense and that in the event of your being killed or wounded in impending operations, or for any other reason, no charge of any kind will fall on British Army funds.

UNWANTED COVERAGE

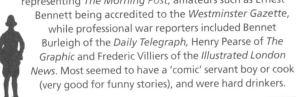

'Get out of my way, you drunken swabs,' is how Kitchener lambasted the war correspondents on the eve of Omdurman. Like many soldiers, he had a disdain for the gentlemen of the Press. They were a mixed bunch; 17 of them were on the battlefield, with soldiers like Churchill representing *The Morning Post*, amateurs such as Ernest Bennett being accredited to the *Westminster Gazette*, while professional war reporters included Bennet Burleigh of the *Daily Telegraph,* Henry Pearse of *The Graphic* and Frederic Villiers of the *Illustrated London News*. Most seemed to have a 'comic' servant boy or cook (very good for funny stories), and were hard drinkers.

March to Omdurman

On 24 August 1898 the final inexorable advance began towards Omdurman along the west bank of the Nile in a double line of brigades with the British nearest the river. The vast front was screened by cavalry and horse artillery and each brigade (except the 4th Egyptians) was followed by a field artillery battery. Behind the troops, stretching across the desert, followed the baggage and supply trains, while the far right flank was protected by the Camel Corps. On the opposite side of the Nile the east bank was similarly guarded by 2500 Arab irregulars commanded by Major E. Montagu-Stuart-Wortley (who had been with Wilson on that fateful day at Khartoum over 13 years earlier). Steaming up the river at a steady pace was a flotilla of 10 gunboats and 5 auxiliary steamers groaning under the weight of two months supply of ammunition and food. When one officer protested that his steamer was overloaded a cheeky Kitchener laconically replied, 'Plimsoll's dead!'

The soldiers suffered badly at first from the summer heat but later encountered rain. Neville Lyttelton, commanding the 2nd British Brigade, noted the march was 'abominably hot over deep

25. Cheerful Cameron Highlanders advancing towards Omdurman.

black sand, and a good many men fell out.' Exactly one week after setting out the Anglo-Egyptian army reached Sururab, just six miles north of the Karari ridges near Omdurman.

That same afternoon, 31 August, the Khalifa Abdullahi reviewed his army on the parade ground near his capital. That night, as the dervishes camped in a vast semi-circle facing north, Abdullahi told his generals that he wanted a great offensive battle. He had decided to divide his army into two main units attacking from different directions; Shaykh al-Din's *mulazimin* would advance towards the enemy until within rifle range while the Black Flag troops, forming a right angle to the riflemen, would attack from the west. It was, said the Khalifa, a return to classic Mahdist warfare. No longer would he meet the infidels in defensive positions, such as Abu Hamed or the Atbara, but in the glory of an offensive charge. They would fall on the unbelievers as they had Hicks at Shaykan, Baker at El Teb and Gordon at Khartoum. If the British formed their defensive squares then the faithful would pierce them just as they had done at Tofrek and Abu Klea. It would be the greatest day in the history of Mahdiism, blessings be unto Allah.

27. A quartet of war correspondents. Left to right: Bennet Burleigh (Daily Telegraph); Rene Bull, (Black and White); Frederic Villiers (Illustrated London News); and Hamilton Weldon (Morning Post).

1 September 1898 – Day of the Gunboats

A terrific downpour saw the British troops thoroughly doused on the night of 31 August and morning of 1 September. Dawn found the men standing, as they had been for at least two hours, thoroughly wet and miserable with a chilly wind blowing.

In Omdurman, after early prayers, the Khalifa prepared to lead his army into battle. Loud shouts of 'Allah Akbar' and the cries of the women helped to drown the distant sound of gunfire as Colin Keppel led his gunboats to attack the dervish river forts. Abdullahi took a position in the centre of his vast host. Shortly before setting off, the wily Osman Digna had drawn the Khalifa's attention to his exposed right flank near the river and, as a result, he now guarded this with his men as well as the line of retreat.

That morning Stuart-Wortley's irregulars seized two villages on the east bank of the Nile and saw some stiff fighting. But, as Sir Philip Magnus has written, 1 September was principally 'the day

A BICYCLE MADE FOR ONE

Hard to believe but true – a British bicycle was wheeled to Omdurman! This belonged to the war correspondent, Frederic Villiers. He even rode his dull green roadster occasionally on the march and others marvelled at the strength of its rubber tyres. Most of the later stages he did on the back of a donkey while his faithful native servant somehow steered both bike and beast. Villiers reasoning was quite cunning – he planned to use the machine just after the battle, cycle across the desert to the Nile and get his sketches and reports onto any boats going down river to Cairo ahead of his rivals.

of the gunboats.' The dervishes fought back but with little chance of success against the new high explosive shells. 'These shells,' wrote the war correspondent, Frederic Villiers,

> … and the projectiles from our twelve pounders were responsible for overwhelming slaughter of Dervishes who stuck to their guns within the forts. Yet some held on to their batteries with remarkable pluck, for when, apparently, a fort had long since been silenced, a puff of smoke and whizz of a shell, coming as it were from a heap of ruins, would astonish us all … On entering some of the forts after the fight, so mangled were the remains of the brave defenders that it was difficult for the moment to recognise that the scattered remains were human flesh.

During the mid-afternoon some well-aimed shells smashed a large hole in the dome of the Mahdi's tomb. The blast was spectacular, the first occasion on which lyddite had been used in action by the British Army.

At 2.05pm the Khalifa halted his army after it had crossed the dry watercourse of Khor Shambat. There was a mighty shout of 'Allah Akbar' and a thunderous discharge into the sky from thousands of rifles. The enemy was not much more than four miles away. About four more hours of daylight were left so it seems likely that Abdullahi intended to rest his troops while deciding whether to spring a night or dawn attack.

Much earlier that day, at 5.00am, the Anglo-Egyptian cavalry had emerged from their zariba at Egeiga, 6.5 miles from Omdurman, to form a crescent guarding the camp and right flank. Moving out they found the low range of the Karari Hills undefended by the enemy. From here, looking south-east, was the river and eight miles beyond they could see the confluence of the Blue and White Niles near Tuti Island. The ruined city of Khartoum was in the far distance. Ahead, to their right, on the west bank of the Nile, lay a large town of mud brick buildings, its skyline dominated by the dome of the Mahdi's tomb. This was Omdurman. Between Omduman and the Karari Hills was what Churchill called a 'spacious amphitheatre' of hard ochre sand with patches of course grass, broken only by occasional small dry watercourses. Three miles south, standing alone, was a high hill called Jebel Surgham. At its base was a long ridge that ran westwards concealing the ground beyond.

From his vantage point Churchill saw a sight that he later described as 'awe-inspiring and formidable'. The dervish ansar was four miles wide as it moved across the sands; masses of horsemen were galloping about, hundreds of banners waved and the sun glinted off thousands of spear points, 'a sparkling

---

OLD ENEMIES, NEW FRIENDS

The Jaalin tribe were the main 'friendlies' who helped the British in 1898. Thirteen years earlier, under Sheikh Ibrahim Farah, they had charged the British squares at Abu Klea and Abu Kru, but times had changed. The Khalifa Abdullahi, while imposing his authority, had tortured and executed 67 of them, and the tribe swore a blood vengeance.

cloud'. An Egyptian Army officer described the sound of the advancing host as 'a dull roar like surf beating on a seashore'. Churchill estimated the enemy 'at not less than forty thousand men'. Colonel Martin, commanding the 21st Lancers, chose him as galloper to make a report to the Sirdar. Trying not to exhaust his horse, but aware of the urgent importance of his task, Churchill cantered up to Kitchener 40 minutes later. It seems that the Sirdar did not recognise him, which was just as well. 'How long do you think I have got?' he asked the young officer. At least half an hour, Churchill replied, then added, 'Probably an hour and a half sir, even if they come on at the present rate.'

Archibald Hunter had also seen the enemy; 'At noon, from the slopes of Jebel Surgham, I saw the entire Dervish army some three miles off advancing towards us, the Khalifa's black flag surrounded by his *Mulazimin* [bodyguard] being plainly discernible. I estimated the number at 35,000 men.' Douglas Haig put the number at 30,000 and noted how, as each *rub* responded to the call to arms, it set off across the desert 'moving very fast indeed'. It was Haig's job to use his cavalry in rear-guard to shepherd the Camel Corps and Maxims back to the British camp. 'The dervish infantry was coming on in lines, running and shouting and beating drums,' and Haig's men had to deal with a 'hot fire' from the dervish riflemen as well as watch their backs when enemy cavalry got 'uncomfortably near'.

The speed of the Mahdists caught the Anglo-Egyptians unawares. A call to arms meant hastily bolted food, packing up and the troops ready for battle by 2.00pm. 'Then the whole army marched out,' wrote Lieutenant Meiklejohn, 'and took up position in a huge semi-circle about 500 yards outside the village, and sat down and waited.' There was muttering in the ranks that 'They ain't got it in 'em; cowards, that's what they are!' But, Meiklejohn noted, 'At dusk we got orders that all lights were to be out by 7.30pm and no smoking after that.' Exact Mahdist figures are arguable but approximately 45,000 dervishes, the cream of the Khalifa'a army, now faced, at about four miles distance, an Anglo-Egyptian force of 25,800 troops with 44 guns and 20 Maxims on land, and 36 guns and 24 Maxims on the Nile. More than 10,000 animals – horses, camels, donkeys and mules – supported the armies.

The day of reckoning had come, except it was possible that it would be a night time engagement. That was Kitchener's greatest fear. Behind a thin zariba of mimosa thorn protecting the British troops (the Egyptians were resting in shallow trenches), the men slept, or stared into the night waiting for the dervish attack, while others wondered if it would be their last day on earth and looked east for the first streaks of dawn.

FIRST PHASE OF THE BATTLE

Night Attack?

The leading Sudanese historian of the Battle of Omdurman, Ismat Zulfo, has written that one dervish scouting party 'made its way unmolested', under cover of darkness, right the way up to Kitchener's camp. They then reported back to the Khalifa.

It had been an unsettling day for Abdullahi; the destruction of the Mahdi's tomb had shocked and angered him. He also knew that such a portent on the eve of the battle would have a bad effect on morale. He had witnessed the deadly power of high explosives and machine guns. Now, as he tried to decide on his final plans, Kitchener's Nile steamers sent brilliant shafts of light periodically through his camp. Osman Azrak, thinking the Khalifa's white tent might make a perfect target, kicked it to the ground.

It seems most likely that when Abdullahi rested his troops early on the afternoon of 1 September he was still considering a night attack. That was what Osman Digna, Ibrahim al Khalil and the other senior commanders urged. That he decided against such sound advice probably saved the Anglo-Egyptian Army – if not from total destruction, then from a terrible fiasco. Archibald Hunter wrote privately after the battle:

CAUGHT ON CAMERA

Omdurman was the first major British battle to be photographed while the action was going on. Rene Bull of the *Black & White*, a pictorial magazine, attempted to take pictures at the Atbara and was even busier on 2 September 1898. Frederic Villiers even had a prototype motion picture camera but no cine film seems to have survived. Two rivals wired for something similar from Cairo and got sent a lantern projector and some saucy slides!

My conviction till I die will be that if he had attacked us in the dark before dawn with the same bravery he attacked us next day by daylight, we should have been pierced, divided, broken & rolled into the river. Few people can realise … what happens when an enemy gets inside your formation. Friend kills friend, contrary orders are given, bugles are sounded to everyone's confusion. All is dark & dust & roar of animals & shrieks of dying & wounded & clamour of natives & shrill yells of enemy & curses & prayers & a Babel of confusion and horror.

Brigadier Lyttelton agreed and thought the Sirdar's disposition weak:

I was up several times in the night and talking to Howard, Commanding the Rifle Brigade, and I asked him how near the Dervishes could come unobserved if they advanced quietly; he thought, and I agreed with him, about 200 yards. This against Egyptian troops in the open with no zariba, would have been very dangerous. Our distribution, too, was obviously faulty; the Egyptians, the inferior troops, armed with the single shooting rifle, ought to have been in the strongest position, the British with magazine rifles on the more exposed unprotected centre and flank.

THE SPYMASTER

Reginald Wingate had commanded part of the 1885 Sudan withdrawal and was to be intimately connected with the country for the next 31 years. Skilled in oriental languages and with a sharp brain, he brilliantly orchestrated the press and public relations campaign to popularise the re-conquest. His intelligence system was first-class, even feeding misinformation to the Mahdist high command on the eve of the battle. Following Omdurman he replaced Kitchener as the Sirdar of the Egyptian Army.

Churchill told a brother officer it would be 'touch and go' on the morrow and went to sleep thinking of the Isandlwana disaster in the 1879 Zulu War.

Kitchener, it appears, was aware that his careful planning could be undone but was attuned to the risk. His brother, Walter, complained:

> I could see nothing that could prevent their getting through our weak lines and once well amongst us there would have been the most hideous melee ever seen. I asked Herbert about it next day, and to my astonishment he admitted at once, 'O yes! I think they would have got through us.'

Intelligence chief Wingate had sent spies to the dervish camp falsely warning of a British attack. The night also had a full moon and this, as much as anything else, probably led Abdullahi to delay his attack until first light.

Reveille

At 3.40am reveille sounded in the Anglo-Egyptian camp. The troops, many of whom had slept fitfully on damp ground, were all fully dressed. There had been a false alarm and call to arms at 1.00am

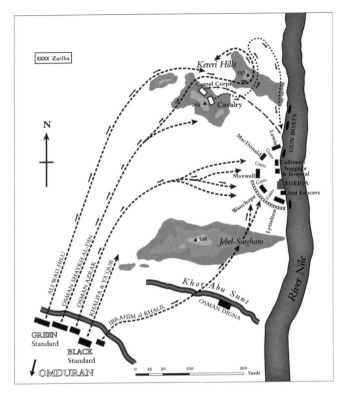

The Battle of Omdurman, First Phase.

but the soldiers had settled down again. It was light by 5.30am 'so we made gaps in the zariba to advance through,' recalled Lieutenant Meiklejohn, 'while the cooks prepared breakfast.'

The Sudanese historian Zulfo wrote that the Egyptian cavalry left the camp at 3.00am but this is not substantiated by other authorities. In his diary, Douglas Haig reports a single squadron of cavalry being sent to reconnoitre at 5.00am, while the rest of the mounted troops moved out at 5.30am – 'cavalry nine squadrons, Camel Corps six companies, four Maxim and horse artillery batteries moved to Karari Ridge, the 21st Lancers to Signal Hill and the infantry paraded by brigades in front of the camp.'

Kitchener next ordered 'a movement on Omdurman in echelon of brigades from the left', but at 5.45am Bimbashi the Honourable Everard Baring, who had led the early reconnaissance, reported back personally to say that 'the whole dervish army was in movement northwards, its right two miles from the river' and its shoulder would probably touch Jebel Surgham where the 21st Lancers had taken up a position.

Mahdist Battle Plan

Then, as now, when a vast ansar was seen streaming across the British front, it confused people. In his cavalry history Lord Anglesey wrote that 'the Khalifa, for some unexplained reason, seems to have assumed that the Sirdar had abandoned his riverside camp.'

The dervishes had a plan. It was flexible, highly suitable to the terrain and depended on timing and the enemy's response. Unfortunately for them, there was no way of knowing how the invaders would react. The plan was for Osman Azrak and his mulazamin to advance as far as Jebel Surgham and then turn directly towards the British camp and attack it frontally. This would be supported by a flank attack on the British lines at the same time led by Ibrahim al Khalil. These two ansar represented about two-fifths of the total strength of the dervish army gathered on the battlefield. What confused some observers (and historians such as Lord Anglesey), was that simultaneous to this assault the mulazamin under Shaykh al-Din, the Khalifa's son, were to occupy

ALL ABOARD HISTORY

It is still possible to stand on an object that was at the Battle of Omdurman and is hardly unchanged. This is Kitchener's steamer, *Melik*, one of the three twin-screw vessels sent out to the Sudan in 1898. Today it is the headquarters of the Blue Nile Sailing Club. It is hoped parts to restore the vessel can be sent from England.

the far-off Karari Hills and wait. The Green Flag troops were to fall in behind this body, while the Black Flag also waited, a reserve for the first phase warriors if they were successful. Abdullahi hoped the first attack would deliver a knockout blow or 'act as bait' to draw the enemy into the claws of his pincers.

The Dervish Army Stirs

At about 4.30am the Khalifa led his army of more than 40,000 in morning prayers. For at least one quarter of them it would be the last day of their lives. Abdullahi stood on an elevation near the Black Flag, 'took out his sword and brandished it three times in the direction of the river and the enemy', calling out 'Allah Akbar'. News reached him that the 'Turks' were on the move. Quickly the army, beating its drums, began to march. At 5.20am, two miles from Jebel Surgham, the left flank and centre block of Green Flag and Shaykh al-Din's warriors set off across the wide plain, right across the front of Kitchener's army some four miles away. Their target was the Karari Hills some ten miles off. While Osman Azrak's ansar moved to fall directly towards the British camp the warriors of Ibrahim al Khalil, some 4000 men, stopped first to head straight up and over Jebel Surgham and fall onto Wauchope's and Lyttelton's British end of the enemy camp.

The 21st Lancers in Danger

Two cavalry patrols, led by Lieutenants Churchill and Smyth, were near the top of Jebel Surgham. It was an overcast morning and in dismal dawn light both officers realised that the dervishes were moving fast towards the hill and enemy horsemen were in the vanguard. 'Bullets whistling & splashing on rocks very close,' noted Smyth, 'Col hearing this sends for me to retire at once … much excited & annoyed & saying I was unnecessarily exposing myself.' Smyth obeyed Colonel Martin but not so Churchill who had to be sent two messages to retire. He was, in fact, lucky to get back into the zariba before the first British volley. The 32nd Field Battery Royal Artillery had opened fire minutes earlier, at 6.45am, shelling dervishes some 2800 yards distant. Soon the rest of the artillery and gunboats joined in the action; early shells went too high but once the gunners had found their range they began cutting swathes in the dervish ranks. Churchill, transfixed, saw some shells

> ... burst in the air, others in their faces, others in the sand and dashed clouds of red dust and splinters amid their ranks. The white flags toppled over ... yet they rose up again as other men pressed forward to die for Allah's sacred cause ... It was a terrible sight for as yet they had not hurt us at all, and it seemed an unfair advantage.

28. The initial charge of the Mahdist army.

Ibrahim al Khalil's Assault

Close on Churchill's heels the first wave of Ibrahim al Khalil's men reached the summit of Jebel Surgham at about 6.40am and then streamed down the other side towards the British. They fired their rifles as they jogged along without thinking of distance, height or aim. When gaps opened up in their ranks their commanders screamed for men to fill them. Emir Ibrahim had covered a quarter of the way from the ridge to the zariba when his horse was hit and collapsed. Mounting his second steed, called 'End', the Emir rode to within 800 yards when he was hit in the chest and head at about 7.05am. Four brave horsemen dismounted, following dervish custom, and carried his body off the battlefield as bullets fell around them. Fifteen minutes later the Maxims had torn such holes in the ansar that what was left of Ibrahim al Khalil's force turned to the left and tried to join Osman Azrak's attack.

Death of Osman Azrak

The Emir Osman Azrak had launched his attack with fire from his riflemen and cannon. Things improved a little for the dervishes when the front line stopped long enough to fire with some accuracy at British troops standing by the zariba some 1600– 2000 yards away. Kitchener, sensing activity by his stretcher bearers, stopped his horse before Wauchope's 1st Brigade and ordered up more artillery.

Realising that death stared him in the face, but determined to rally his ranks, Osman Azrak led 50 horsemen and 100 foot soldiers in a mad dash towards the zariba. With bullets raining down, the Emir fell about 400 yards short of his goal. Bravely carrying his standard a bearer and five dismounted horsemen continued to charge until mown down by the British fire. Three hundred other warriors under a commander called Ibrahim Jabir got to a sandy depression 500 yards from the British 1st Brigade's lines, carefully took aim and managed to hit about 50 of the enemy. This victory of sorts was all the more remarkable when one realises how antiquated their weapons were and that the morning sunlight was shining in their eyes. In exasperation Wauchope was thinking of asking for cavalry support when, at 7.55am, artillery began shelling the dervish position made discernible by its battle standard. Ibrahim Jabir was wounded in the stomach while most of his unit were wiped out. The first two Mahdist ansar had been annihilated by 8.00am with a loss of roughly 3000 dead and 4000 wounded. The Anglo-Egyptians had lost 5 officers and 155 men dead and wounded in this first phase.

The British Brigades

Many soldiers were glad when the dervishes finally attacked. The big battle was at last on. 'Get into your places please, gentlemen, the show is starting,' is how the adjutant of the Warwicks rallied his officers. The Grenadier Guards, at 2000 yards range, are credited with being the first British regiment to open fire, at

29. Kitchener observes and directs his battle from a small mound.

In The Khalifa's Clutches

Over the years the Mahdists had captured and imprisoned several Europeans. Besides the Austrian, Rudolph von Slatin, who escaped from Omdurman, another escapee was Father Joseph Ohrwalder, who got away in 1891. Others held there in 1898 included Guiseppe Cuizzi, former British consular agent at Berber, George Stambouli, a Christian Syrian who converted to Islam and Pietro Agati, an Italian bricklayer who built the Khalifa's house. Re-plastered, the building is largely unchanged in Omdurman and today is a memorial to the Khalifa's memory.

6.50am, followed by the Highlanders and Lincolns. Company volley fire was permitted at 1500 yards. Officers shouted out the commands – 'Ready' – 'Present' – 'Fire'. Later, sergeants and colour sergeants directed half companies and sections as the men fired up to twelve rounds a minute. This was close order, line formation, exactly as at Waterloo, in two lines, front rank kneeling, rear rank standing. At 800 yards the battle raged all along the British lines. Colour-Sergeant Fraley, Rifle Brigade, watched a group of dervishes heading towards him: 'First one man dropped, then the fellow carrying the flag, another picked it up and still came on, when the two left almost dropped together, they marched straight to death right enough.' A few Mahdist shells from Osman Azrak's guns reached the zariba; one landed amongst the Camerons, one did damage amongst the Seaforths and at least two fell in the Egyptian ranks.

Ernest Bennett, correspondent of *The Westminster Gazette*, was astounded by the din: 'The roar of the artillery, the shriek of shells, the crisp volleys of the Lee-Metfords and the unceasing rat-tat-tat of the deadly Maxims.' Added to these sounds were the drums and chants of the dervishes, especially their cry, 'La Illah illa'llah wa Muhammad rasal Allah' – 'There is but one God and Muhammad is his Prophet.'

Several men had lucky escapes. Ernest Bennett noted how a dervish bullet 'bored a hole through the helmet of the man in front, tore through the shoulder-strap of the man behind, then wounded a sergeant in the leg, and finally dropped harmlessly on the toes of a private in the rear.' Another Tommy found a bullet had gone into his haversack and buried itself in his prayer book.

Fight in the Karari Hills

While the battle raged on the plain another fight was going on in the Karari Hills. At about 6.50am, just as the British artillery opened fire, Shaykh al-Din's men began climbing up the hills 'at a great pace'. Broadwood, with his cavalry, found his artillery and galloping Maxims 'had not the slightest effect in checking them'.

30. One of the gunboat crews in action on the Nile.

The Sirdar, aware of the danger, ordered Broadwood to disengage and retire towards the zariba. Fearing that the dervishes might follow pell mell and attack the Anglo-Egyptian lines at the northern and weakest end, Broadwood chose to ignore Kitchener's command. Instead he led his cavalry with the enemy on his heels some way northwards in a fighting withdrawal. During this dogfight the Camel Corps, despite horse artillery support, suffered over 60 casualties. Artillerymen, 'two on a horse or clinging to the stirrups of a friend', fled leaving two guns behind. Luckily for the Camel Corps, the howitzers of the steamer *Melik*, commanded by 'Monkey' Gordon, saved them.

Meanwhile Haig's troopers, in a continual repetition of dismounting, firing, mounting again and riding a short distance, held off many attackers despite 'a very hot fire'. The dervishes gave up this wild goose chase over the west portion of the Karari Hills at about 8.00am and some Egyptian cavalry rode back and reclaimed their guns, while the rest trotted south to re-join the infantry. The next day a British officer counted 1185 dead dervishes on the ridge.

At the Egyptian Trenches

It was Maxwell's brigade who bore the brunt of the first attack on the Egyptian defences. Townshend, commanding the 12th Sudanese, refused to let his men fire until the dervishes were 600 yards away, though due to the Martini-Henry's slower rate of fire compared to the Lee Metford, some warriors got to within 300 yards distance. Lewis, commanding the 3rd Egyptian Brigade, realised 'This was no horde of savages but a well-ordered army.' It was independent firing. 'Struck by a leaden tempest, they *bundled* over in heaps,' recalled Townshend, and finally slunk back, though none ran. 'Their retirement was a haughty stalk of offended dignity,' thought Major Bagot, Grenadier Guards. In total the British and Egyptian infantry expended 200,000 rounds of ammunition in about one hour's fighting (over 3000 rounds a minute).

31. A rare photograph of Maxwell (mounted) talking with an aide just a few minutes before the initial dervish attack. Note the Egyptian troops resting or kneeling in their zariba trench.

Dervish Bravery

Captain Eadon, 21st Lancers, watched Ibrahim al Khalil's men attack and wrote that they were 'too magnificent for words … I could see the shells dropping into their dense masses and killing heaps at a shot, but they still advanced.' Part of the grisly fascination at Omdurman was due to the smokeless powder of the Lee-Metford rifles. There was no swirling smoke to prevent observers from experiencing the full horror of the violence the new firepower could unleash. War correspondent G.W. Steevens was unequivocal that 'no white troops could have faced that torrent of death for five minutes.' He watched one old man, carrying a white standard, who refused to give up, even when his comrades collapsed, until he was 200 yards from the 14th Sudanese. 'Then he folded his arms across his face, and his limbs loosened, and he dropped sprawling to earth beside his flag.'

A similar old warrior died facing the Warwicks. When the sound of gunfire ceased and the lone old dervish had crumpled to the ground a ranker spoke out: 'That was a *man*. These black chaps know how to fight and how to die.'

THE CHARGE OF THE 21ST LANCERS

In the interim between the first phase of the battle and its decisive second part there occurred an incident that has long overshadowed both – the charge of the 21st Lancers. This event has been dismissed as a sideshow with little bearing on the main action, yet it remains the single most memorable fighting of the whole day and was the last full regimental charge of British cavalry.

At 7.30am General Gatacre galloped up to Lieutenant-Colonel Rowland Martin and the rest of the 21st Lancers who were grouped by the Nile at the zariba's southern tip. He told the regiment to go out on a second reconnaissance towards Jebel Surgham and study enemy dispositions on the plain and their line of retreat; if the 21st reported the route towards Omdurman was clear then the infantry would follow.

A few shots were fired at them by stragglers in the desert and riflemen high up on the hill but Martin got his regiment beneath Jebel Surgham by 8.15am. The signals officer, Lieutenant Clerk, climbed high enough to send a message from Martin to the Sirdar, at considerable risk to himself. It said fresh dervish troops were retiring towards Omdurman. One can only guess at Kitchener's reaction to this news; could this be the rest of the Khalifa's army seen just before the dervish onslaught, or at least a large portion of it, moving back into the city? Would he now face a deadly assault on the streets of Omdurman from Abdullahi's crack riflemen?

Not sure exactly how to interpret Martin's news, but certainly not wanting dervish warriors to enter Omdurman, the Sirdar sent a message back at 8.30am: 'To Colonel Martin. Annoy them as far as possible on their flank and head them off if possible from Omdurman. Sirdar.' Martin, upon reading this note, decided to ignore the scores of dervish wounded fleeing towards the city, but disperse any units of enemy troops lying in that direction. The historian of the charge has written that, 'The order clearly changed the regiment's primary task from reconnaissance to engagement.'

Moving off towards the south, Martin sent ahead two patrols under Lieutenants Grenfell and Pirie. There is some confusion over whether Gatacre told Martin to search for the Khalifa's reserve army south-west of the hill. Grenfell's patrol trotted in that direction but was forced to turn back due to heavy sniper fire from the summit. Events might have been totally different if that patrol had not been distracted because, as Pirie led his men south towards the Omdurman road, keeping a distance of about 100 yards from retreating dervish wounded, he spotted what appeared to be 1000 of the enemy (his trumpeter reckoned 700) blocking the advance. Quickly Pirie turned his patrol around and

32. A rare photograph of the 21st Lancers shortly before the famous charge, resting by the slopes of Jebel Surgham.

reported back to Lieutenant-Colonel Martin. The 21st now moved from a walk to a trot and headed towards the enemy.

What the 21st did not know was that they were heading into a trap planned by a true master of desert warfare – Osman Digna. It was to be a last gift for his enemies and the final example of his expertise in delivering an ambush. Philip Ziegler has written: 'It was one of the oldest and favourite tricks in the Arab repertoire; Broadwood would have been immediately suspicious, Martin had no such qualms.'

Osman Digna's Ambush

Lieutenant Pirie had spied a low ridge covered with warriors. What he did not see was that beyond and hidden by them was a dry watercourse, Khor Abu Sunt, that dropped six to eight feet from the plain. Seven hundred of Osman Digna's loyal fuzzy-haired Hadendowa warriors, mostly armed with knives and spears, were waiting to surprise the British.

Seeing the British cavalry on the move, reinforcements swiftly and silently entered the khor from its Jebel Surgham spur until there were something over 2000 of them (British accounts normally say 2800, but Zulfo gives a lower estimate, and as he talked with dervish participants at Omdurman, I am inclined to accept his figure).

Riflemen, about 150 of them, stood on the northern rim of the khor, so as to be seen, while the bulk sat in the dry watercourse, 12–20 men deep and extending for 400 yards eastwards. Zulfo is adamant that the Khalifa watched the ensuing action from an angle of the khor to the British right flank. Some modern historians have disputed Abdullahi's presence but, once again, Zulfo had the benefit of talking with battle survivors. Osman Digna (in talks with H.C. Jackson during his captivity many years later), also confirmed that the Khalifa was there.

The Charge

Lieutenant-Colonel Martin was well aware that his force of over 400 officers and men was more than sufficient to dislodge 1000 dervishes. By the time the 21st got to within sight of the enemy, Pirie's '1000' had dwindled, in the words of Major Finn, to 'a couple of hundred Dervishes on a slight eminence'. Lieutenant Smyth confirmed the same. Riding from the north, Martin decided to take his time and examine the enemy; he wheeled his regiment to the left into columns of troops (each troop followed by the next) and trotted along facing the dervishes at about 300 yards. There is a possibility that he was turning over in his mind the option of dislodging them from a distance with carbine fire. Whatever his thoughts, a withering fusillade from the dervish riflemen (crack shots from the Khalifa's bodyguard), probably helped Martin decide on a charge. Lieutenant de Montmorency, B Squadron, spoke for many when he shouted out, 'Why the blazes don't we charge those … before they shoot us down?' Raised as the 3rd Bengal European Light Cavalry after the Mutiny, re-designated the 21st Light Dragoons, then made a hussar regiment, later still a lancer one, Martin was distinctly aware that his corps had no battle honours and no real glory. Anyway, as one officer said, they were not mounted infantry, but lancers and the Sirdar had clearly ordered them to 'annoy' the enemy. The colonel called out 'Right Wheel into line'. His 16 troops swung perfectly into one long line. The total, now trotting along, were 34 officers, 412 men and one civilian (Hubert Howard, correspondent of *The Times*). The line also included Captain the Marquess of Tullibardine, ADC to the Sirdar, who had galloped up to assess the situation just seconds earlier.

The charge itself happened naturally – no calls for 'canter', 'gallop' or 'charge' were ever sounded. In the lead, 30 yards ahead of his regiment, rode Rowland Martin. It took about half a minute's hard riding to reach the enemy with D and B Squadrons in the centre and C and A at the left and right flanks. Martin was

33. Captain Paul Kenna VC, 21st Lancers.

so preoccupied looking over his shoulder, urging on his men, that he forgot to draw his sword or revolver. Most officers held their swords out in pointed cavalry style known as 'riding down the blade', but Major Fowle, B Squadron and Lieutenant Churchill, A Squadron, both waved the latest Mauser semi-automatic pistols instead of standard-issue Webley revolvers. One officer, Captain Kenna, charged lance in hand like his men. Raymond de Montmorency, head down, thought the bullets were a 'hailstorm, with a continuous "whizz", "whizz", "whizz" and an occasional clink as a bullet hit a sword or lance point.'

Between 100 and 50 yards from the khor the massed spearmen, now standing upright, became visible to the speeding horsemen. They also saw small groups of dervishes sitting patiently on the sands waiting to hamstring the horses with their knives. It was suddenly clear to all that they were riding into a trap. 'Men frantically spurred their horses on to gain the greatest possible momentum, which alone might carry them through and out the other side.'

In the Khor

The shock effect of over 400 horsemen travelling at about 20 miles an hour, each horse and rider weighing up to half a ton, must have been tremendous as the 21st Lancers pummelled into the front ranks of the enemy. Churchill wrote that 'they all fell knocked A.O.T. (arse over tip). One man in my troop fell. He was cut to pieces.' Several dervishes were spitted on the nine-foot lances and carried backwards into the khor.

First in, Lieutenant-Colonel Martin was almost unhorsed but rode through the melee unscathed. Less lucky was his second-in-command, Major Crole-Wyndham, who landed on his feet after his horse was shot. He had to make an escape 'slashing and firing' as dervishes surrounded him. Quickly the khor filled with the rest

34. Beja friendlies – the curly-haired Hadendowa are the same tribe that slaughtered the 21st Lancers.

35. Lieutenant the Honourable Raymond de Montmorency VC, 21st Lancers.

of the regiment and it was in this dense mass of horses and men that the tribesmen were able to do their deadliest work. In such a scrum the lance proved to be a useless weapon, one officer's sword bent double and another 'snapped on striking a dervish spear.' Luckily for the officers and sergeants, they were also armed with revolvers.

Crole-Wyndham, incredibly, got out of the khor on foot and ran off only to find himself stalked by a lone dervish horseman. He was saved by Lieutenant de Montmorency, who shot the man in the back and then bravely returned to the khor to retrieve the body of Lieutenant Grenfell, B Squadron (a nephew of the former Sirdar), who had fallen from his horse and been hacked to death. Earlier Montmorency had lost his own horse and been saved by the swift intervention of Captain Paul Kenna and Corporal F. Swarbrick.

Another unseated officer, Lieutenant Molyneux, C Squadron, was saved by Private Thomas Byrne, B Squadron (who had been the last man to enter the khor). Without his lance and wounded

36. The last full regimental charge of British cavalry.

37. Private Thomas Byrne VC, 21st Lancers.

in his sword arm, Byrne was on his way out when he heard Molyneux's cry for help and replied, 'All right, Sir, I won't leave you!' He gave the officer precious seconds to escape by riding into four nearby dervishes and battering them with his horse. Byrne lost his sword and was wounded a second time by a spear thrust in his chest.

The fight in the khor lasted barely three minutes yet for all 447 men who charged it was the most action-packed 180 seconds of their lives. Lieutenant Robert Smyth, A Squadron, entered the watercourse where it was less congested, yet his account is riven with breathless energy:

> Find myself at khor, man bolts out leaving 2 donkeys in my way, catch hold of horse hard by head, knowing to fall would be fatal. He blunders against donkey, recovers & scrambles out. Am met by swordsman on foot, cuts at my right front, I guard it with sword. Next man, fat face, all in white, having fired & missed me, throws up both hands, I cut him across the face, he drops. Large bearded man in blue with 2 edged sword in both hands cuts at me, think this time I must be done but pace tells & my guard carries it off. Duck my head to spear thrown, just misses me. Another cut at my horse, miss guard but luckily cut is too far away & only cuts through my breast-plate & gives my horse a small flesh-wound … Rally my troop as well as I can. Horrible sights, everyone seems to be bleeding … It seems to be blood, blood, blood everywhere, horses & men smothered, either their own or other people's. Wounded men being carried off by others, as one sees in pictures, horses dropping down & being carried away.

The 21st Re-group

By 9.50am the 21st had re-grouped. Martin now considered a second charge to recover any wounded but decided the risk of further losses was too great. The dervishes, elated by their success, looked ready to advance. The Colonel, as Churchill cheekily quipped, 'remembered for the first time that he had carbines'; troopers led by Lieutenant Taylor, C Squadron, began firing and the enemy slowly fell back, but in good order, taking their wounded with them. Two hours later a British officer counted 21 dead dervishes in the khor. The British had lost 1 officer and 20 men slain and 50 officers and men wounded, along with 119 horses killed or badly injured.

Reactions

The Times called the charge 'an extremely brilliant affair' while *The Daily Mail* dismissed it as 'a gross blunder'. Most war correspondents, naturally enough, likened it to the heroic yet futile Charge of the Light Brigade at Balaklava.

Amongst officers the general view seemed to be that it was 'a very gallant but foolish action'. The waspish Douglas Haig wrote that 'the regiment was keen to do something and meant to charge … I trust for the sake of the British Cavalry that more tactical knowledge exists in the higher ranks of the average regiment than we have seen displayed in this one.' General Sir Frederick Maxse wrote: 'The Lancers' charge was not only unnecessary, but had the greater disadvantage of incapacitating the regiment from the performance of the particular duty it was brought to the Sudan to accomplish – namely the capture of the Khalifa – and the fact that both officers and men behaved with great gallantry is no excuse for a blunder.'

Kitchener was extremely annoyed at the waste of life and Martin's inability to locate the main dervish army. But such courage, as the Sirdar realised, was the kind of 'show' the great British public would appreciate. Walter Kitchener wrote 'Of course the charge was unnecessary … but good work and sound for recruiting.'

The final words deserve to go to the participants; Major Finn said 'there was no choice but to charge or gallop away'; Lieutenant Smyth shared the view 'that we did what we were told

38. The officers of the 21st Lancers, in a photograph taken some days after the battle. Colonel Martin is fourth from left, front row. Next to him (from left) are Majors Crole-Wyndham and Finn. Many of the men wear black armbands to commemorate their dead colleagues.

to do,' though clearly Martin ignored the option of dismounting beforehand, firing on the enemy and sending a patrol around them to see what lay beyond. Churchill, clearly in a minority, thought the charge 'not in the least exciting'. He asked one of his sergeants if he had enjoyed himself: 'Well, I don't exactly say I enjoyed it, Sir,' came the phlegmatic reply, 'but I think I'll get more used to it next time.'

SECOND PHASE
OF THE BATTLE

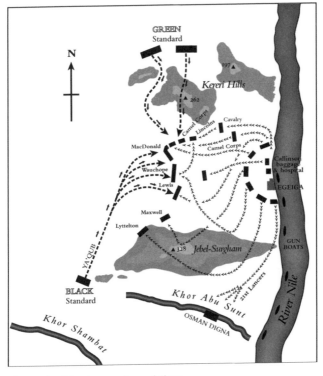

The Battle of Omdurman, Second Phase.

Sirdar Orders the General Advance

When the first attacks had died down at 8.00am the Sirdar's troops were allowed to snatch a second more substantial breakfast. Regiments conducted basic tasks; Lieutenant Meiklejohn of the Warwicks did some quick sums and found that his 70-strong company had already expended 5543 rounds of ammunition.

After 'about an hour' the whole force got orders to march on Omdurman and to expect more fighting. Marching by brigade they were, from the left, commanded by Lyttelton, Wauchope, Maxwell, MacDonald and Lewis (with Collinson's 4th Egyptians in the rear to shepherd the transport). Disarray set in immediately as the two British brigades, both wanting the honour of being first inside Omdurman, set off smartly and quickly outpaced Maxwell in the centre. Precious minutes were lost as Hunter switched the positions of his 3rd and 1st Brigades so that the tough Sudanese were marching on the right flank with the Camel Corps. MacDonald's men had to wait for Lewis's brigade to pass them and a gap nearly a mile wide opened up between them.

A RATHER AMUSING VC

Just as Phase Two of the battle was starting two newsmen, described officially as 'camp followers', were taking snapshots among the dervish dead when a warrior rose up and pursued them with a big spear. Nevill Smyth, one of Hunter's aides, won a Victoria Cross for riding out and killing the dervish. Most authorities do not name the two foolish journalists but Archibald Hunter, in a private letter, says they were Bennet Burleigh and Rene Bull; Bull was definitely taking pictures on the battlefield. One observer said that the whole episode was 'rather amusing' as several shots were fired, 'dangerous to everyone except to the Dervish'.

39. Lieutenant Nevill Smyth, Queen's Bays, who won a Victoria Cross saving the life of two war correspondents.

As the march got underway MacDonald found that his brigade, farthest out in the plain, was alone. He saw dervish spearmen ahead and asked Lewis to help protect his right flank. 'Taffy' Lewis had just got orders to catch up with Maxwell and felt unable to assist MacDonald who then sent a galloper to the Sirdar asking whether he should attack the enemy. Kitchener, according to Hunter, was 'impatient & had bad sight anyhow', so he tetchily replied to the galloper, Lieutenant Pritchard RE, 'Can he not see that we are marching on Omdurman. Tell him to follow on.' The time was 9.30am.

Kitchener's Blunder

Tactics were never Herbert Kitchener's strong point. It is clear that when he ordered an advance his aim was to get to Omdurman as quickly as possible, and to occupy it with the minimum of fuss. He must have been well aware that more than half the Khalifa's army had still not been met on the battlefield, yet vast numbers of them had been sighted streaming across his front just three hours earlier. Where were they? The inescapable conclusion is that he thought Broadwood's cavalry were challenging and disrupting the Green Flag warriors in the Karari Hills and the fresh dervishes spotted by the 21st Lancers moving back towards Omdurman were divisions of the Black Flag. It was thus imperative to set off with haste towards the city and to secure it at the earliest opportunity.

Without proper intelligence, for once Kitchener was taking a huge gamble. He had no way of knowing exactly where the Khalifa's armies were and, as it turned out, he was wrong in his suppositions; the dervishes still wanted a battle – as he was about to discover.

Black Flag Attack

At 9.30am cannon fire was heard to the Anglo-Egyptian right. It was MacDonald encountering the Black Flag ansar under Ya'qub, the Khalifa's brother, the spearmen he had seen in the distance. A flurry of orders from Kitchener to subordinate commanders were now sent: ignoring Gatacre, Hunter and divisional command he ordered Wauchope to change direction and fill the gap between Lewis and MacDonald, the men having to march double-quick under a blazing sun; Lewis was told to direct his artillery on the

A FIGHTING CLERIC

The first ever 'religious DSO' went to Father Robert Brindle, Roman Catholic chaplain to the troops at Omdurman, a great favourite amongst officers and men alike. Brindle had served in other campaigns; on one of these he tried to encourage the soldiers by saying, 'Fire low boys but no swearing please!' One impressed Tommy Atkins said to his mate, 'I like that bloody priest Joe. I'm going to do just what he f*****g says!'

Black Flag while rushing to MacDonald's aid; and Lyttelton and Maxwell were ordered to face west, climb up to the summit of Jebel Surgham and attack the right flank of the enemy as it swept forward. The brigades got on the move and as they spread out the effect resembled 'a long human wall creeping westwards, more than 4000 yards long, a line level with the plain, but with a sudden lurch upwards where the two brigades of Lyttelton and Maxwell were on the summit and slopes.'

The Black Flag ansar was divided into 51 standards of between 25 and 1500 men. Their leaders, besides Ya'qub, included Mohammad al Mahdi, the Mahdi's eldest son. Spread out across the plain the huge army was 4000 yards long and 23 rows deep. Horsemen were at the front and sides but most of the warriors were new recruits. Seeing the body of Ibrahim al Khalil gave Ya'qub inspiration: 'Ansar, look at us now! Young men like

40. The heroic defence of the Khalifa's black banner.

119

Ibrahim al Khalil have gone to their eternal resting place ... Raise your banners aloft and let your horses charge!' He galloped along the whole line of his army shouting encouragement, then turned his horse towards the enemy.

Within minutes the Black Flag charge crumpled beneath a vast line of fire; MacDonald's brigade alone fired 450 shells and Lewis's brigade, arriving for the last 15 minutes of the fight, fired 37,000 rounds of ammunition (well over 2000 rounds a minute). 'The swish of our bullets was like the swish of water,' recalled Pritchard, 'Only one or two horsemen got within 100 yards. The leading Emir was hit twice ... but he still came on at full gallop and was lifting his spear when he fell within 40 yards of our line.' Ya'qub was killed at about 9.35am by a stream of Maxim bullets. Two brave horsemen dismounted to recover his body but they too were mown down. By 10.00am the attack was over.

Khalifa Abdullahi Leaves the Battlefield

From the peak of Jebel Surgham, Lyttelton and Maxwell were able to fire directly on the Khalifa's headquarters down on the plain.

41. Behind the firing line at Omdurman.

The second Khalifa, Ali wad Helu, was hit in the thigh by a bullet that had to be extracted. When Lyttelton's men started to advance the situation became critical and Abdullahi's entourage urged that he retire to Omdurman. But the death of Ya'qub had totally demoralised him. 'So long as you are alive, true religion triumphs,' said one emir. Wishing to console his long-time friend, Osman Digna added, 'This is not the end of everything.' The Khalifa refused to ride his white horse and returned to the capital on a donkey. Once there he ate a frugal meal and then went to the Mahdi's tomb to pray.

Green Flag Attack

No sooner was the Black Flag attack dwindling than MacDonald had to face a new enemy from a fresh direction; tearing down the gullies of the Karari Hills and across the plain came detachments of Uthman al-Din's ansar that had engaged Broadwood's cavalry earlier in the battle. They were supported by the Emir Ali wad Helu's men – more than 15,000 warriors. Unlike the Black Flag these ansar included hundreds of riflemen. At 1200 yards they stopped to fire a volley.

42. MacDonald's brigade going into action.

43. Macdonald's Sudanese repelling the vast Mahdist attack on their brigade.

When an order came from Hunter to withdraw if the pressure got worse, an infuriated MacDonald exclaimed, 'I'll no do it. I'll see them damned first. We maun just fight!' With parade ground skill honed by years as a drill sergeant, bullets whistling around, 'Fighting Mac' barked out a series of orders despite being in severe pain from a broken foot. His brigade made a complete change of its front to meet the new enemy, moving at the double under fire, battalion by battalion, so that it formed 'an arrow-head with a gradually lengthening barb facing almost north.'

The battle was now at its most critical juncture. Had the Black Flag and Green Flag warriors coordinated their attacks, or if MacDonald's Sudanese battalions had faltered, there is no way of knowing what might have happened (some modern historians speculate that Wauchope's brigade could have held off the dervishes, but some of those present that day thought otherwise).

MacDonald's men had been under fire for almost an hour, their rifles almost too hot to hold, while casualties gradually mounted to 168 in the brigade and 40 more in the Camel Corps. Coolly, MacDonald strode up and down his ranks, directing his men's fire, admonishing some of its commanders and proving himself to be the perfect brigadier. It is perhaps fitting that this great display of discipline under fire came from Sudanese fighting their own countrymen.

The dervishes threw themselves boldly into this wall of steel as fire hit them from first MacDonald's brigade and then Wauchope's men, as well as the Nile flotilla. Sixteen times they tried to advance and sixteen times they were mown down. By 11.00am it was virtually over.

Charge of the Baggara Horsemen

With the din dying down and the battlefield strewn with thousands of dead, dying and wounded men and animals a final climactic moment occurred, one so spectacular that many British soldiers watched it in awe and remembered it for the rest of their lives. Some 200 Baggara horsemen, knowing they had no chance of altering the battle's outcome and that they were doomed, decided on a futile but heroic gesture.

'One of the finest things I've ever seen,' said one British officer, 'They hadn't a chance … but not one man faltered, each rode to his death without flinching, a few got so close that officers drew their revolvers but none got up to the line.'

Bimbasi Franks, directing Maxim gun fire on the horsemen was astounded by 'their perfectly magnificent' gallantry.

You never saw anything so stirring and so recklessly brave. These picturesque wild Arabs, absolutely racing to meet death, on and on they came through the hail of bullets as if they had charmed lives. Then suddenly the deadly hail seemed to catch them, like a sudden gale striking a ship, about 200 yards from us … They came on and on till they seemed to melt and finally break to pieces and disappear, leaving nothing but dead strewn like leaves after a storm.

44. The Battle of Omdurman – 'medieval warriors against Maxims'. (The Illustrated London News)

Horace Smith-Dorrien, who had been one of the lucky few to escape the Zulus at Isandlwana 21 years before, thought them 'a sight never to be forgotten ... Not a man reached the line, but only two or three horses galloped riderless through.'

The Sirdar put down his field glasses. He seemed satisfied. 'Well,' he said, 'We have given them a good dusting.'

THIRD PHASE OF THE BATTLE

'Cease Fire'

It was nearly noon and the march towards Omdurman could resume. The war correspondent, Ernest Bennett, borrowed a pair of field glasses.

> I saw a little band of Dervishes – some sixty in all – painfully making their way to the west. I could even see the faces of the poor wretches, the majority of whom seemed to be wounded. Some limped along unaided over the rough hillside, others supported by their comrades. How many hundreds, nay thousands, of these wounded Dervishes ultimately succumbed to the fearful injuries inflicted by the 'man-stopping' bullet, no one, I suppose, will ever know accurately, but one may be tolerably sure that behind the hills many a poor creature lay down to die.

Bimbashi Seymour Vandaleur of the 9th Sudanese rode out after the cease fire sounded to stop his men shooting the wounded. Suddenly a warrior rose up from the plain and ran quickly towards him. 'His first spear whizzed past my head,' recalled Vandaleur, 'I hit him with two revolver bullets but still he closed with me.' The

45. *The dead photographed by Rene Bull within minutes of the ceasefire.*

dervish thrust at the British officer with another spear, wounding him in the hand before being killed by a Sudanese infantryman. Afterwards Vandaleur felt that 'the new man-stopping bullet is not much use against a good Dervish.'

Tired and hot, the British troops set off while Gatacre kept galloping along 'in great excitement' shouting, 'The Khalifa is just in front; you will catch him from behind that ridge.' The heat was intense and the sights and smells truly terrible. 'Bodies of men, horses, donkeys, even a stray camel or two everywhere,' wrote Lieutenant Meiklejohn, 'Some horribly mutilated, a few burning.' Reaching a khor about 2.00pm, the British troops rushed for the water, even though it had several bodies lying in it (several cases of enteric fever in the coming days were ascribed to this incident). 'Later on we marched into Omdurman, the Egyptian bands playing us in,' recalled Meiklejohn, 'Everybody pretty weary. Two or three deaths from sunstroke and one of our men suddenly started singing, went raving mad, and died with five or six men holding him down.' That night the Warwicks camped near the Mahdi's tomb and the officers opened a dozen bottles of champagne, saved for the occasion, and had three-quarters of a pint each. For the Egyptian cavalry, the fighting was not quite over. Ordered to harass the retiring Mahdists, Bimbashi Haig recalled some hot work: 'Many wounded still rose up and fired as we approached, and spearmen tried to hurl a spear … I saw men begging for pardon and then, when we had passed, treacherously assault some unsuspecting trooper from the rear.' At one point a group of dervishes who had flung down their arms picked them up again, 'so that we were enveloped with a cross fire from all directions … It was a ridiculous idea for three squadrons to attack some 10 or more thousands of resolute and armed men all scattered across the plain.' By 3.00pm, when the troopers reached the Nile, Haig had lost five men and nineteen horses wounded.

Sirdar Enters Omdurman

Kitchener entered Omdurman with the captured Black Flag of the Khalifa following behind him. The street was eerily deserted and the doors were all shut until an elderly sheikh appeared and asked the Sirdar if he intended to massacre the women and children. On being assured that nothing of the kind was planned he presented a huge key to Kitchener and within minutes women were screaming a welcome from the rooftops.

46. With the captured banner of the Khalifa the Sirdar prepares to ride into Omdurman town.

47. The damage done to the dome of the Mahdi's tomb by British shellfire.

The British found the city to be quite loathsome; its mud-brick streets 'were all a huge latrine', noted one officer, with over 500 dead bodies and refuse everywhere. 'The smell was beyond words,' and some, like the Grenadier Guards chaplain, vomited.

The inner city and Khalifa's sanctum, known as the Sur, were walled and it was believed that crack Mahdist warriors waited inside to make a final stand but, upon entry, this was found to be untrue. The 13th Sudanese rushed ahead under Smith-Dorrien to search for the Khalifa but there was no trace of him. When the Sirdar reached the Khalifa's house the same troops were busy looting chickens. Hunter recalled that his soldiers 'did have an afternoon, poking into houses, in and out of narrow alleys, kicking down doors, forcing gateways, chasing devils all over the place, most surrendered, but we had to kill some 300 or 400.' Clearly, old scores were settled, though a few die-hards did put up a fight; two attacked Smith-Dorrien in the courtyard of the Khalifa's house, killing a corporal and wounding two others before they were despatched. Hunter admitted, as the night wore on, that his men simply wanted 'the prettiest slave-girls and best trophies'. One suspects several residents died protecting both.

The late afternoon was, in the words of Walter Kitchener, 'most exciting'. Near the Khalifa's house the Sirdar and leading troops found themselves the victims of friendly fire from one of the Nile gunboats. Tragically a splinter killed Hubert Howard, the daredevil war correspondent son of the Earl of Carlisle. A few hours earlier he had ridden with the 21st Lancers and survived their charge unscathed. He was, thought Brigadier Lyttelton, 'the keenest unprofessional soldier I had ever met,' having seen fighting in Cuba and Matabeleland. His death was 'a perverse fatality'. Earlier that day, during the first phase of the battle, Colonel Frank Rhodes, a correspondent for *The Times* (and well-liked brother of

48. Kitchener released hundreds of the Khalifa's prisoners; here Charles Neufeld is found in chains within hours of the British victory.

Cecil), had been wounded. A third journalist, Henry Cross of *The Manchester Guardian*, was already down with enteric fever and later died.

Kitchener finally reached the Khalifa's gaol and made sure that his prisoners were released, including a German, Charles Neufeld, who had been in captivity for eleven years, and Sister Teresa Grigolini, a nun who had been forced to marry.

The Butcher's Bill

That night Kitchener wrote his despatches; 'I thank the Lord of Hosts for giving us victory at so small a cost in our dead and wounded.' The cost had been slight for the Sirdar: 2 British and 2 Egyptian officers killed in action, 29 British Army and 18 Egyptian Army other ranks dead (along with Hubert Howard); 382 of all ranks wounded. During the whole re-conquest fewer than 60 British officers and men had died in action, though as many as 300 more succumbed to disease. Total Egyptian Army losses are

49. The dervish dead lie bloated in the sun on the battlefield.

50. Raising the British and Egyptian flags during the service held amidst the ruins of Gordon's palace at Khartoum.

difficult to judge but about 150 officers and men had been killed in action or died from wounds.

The day after the battle the dervish dead were counted as 10,800; their total wounded will never be known but 20–21,000 seems very likely. In about five hours of fighting the British and Egyptian troops had poured 444,000 bullets at their enemy, the Maxims had used 67,000 rounds and the Mahdists had been blasted with 3500 shells.

On Sunday 4 September a memorial service for Gordon was held amongst the ruins of the Governor-General's palace at Khartoum. All units were represented and officers agreed the ceremony and hoisting of the Union flag and Egyptian flags was 'most impressive'. National anthems were played, as well as Gordon's favourite hymn – 'Abide With Me'. Officers were given twenty minutes to look around. Captain Alfred Hubbard of the Lincolns thought the whole place 'was terribly tumble-down', but 'so cool & refreshing to look at after the glare & sand of the desert'.

Treatment of the Dervish Wounded

That same day all the wounded were taken down river. Major Adamson, Medical Officer of the Lincolns, recalled it as 'a horrible memory … for all along the river edge were dead or wounded dervishes, great vultures tearing at the corpses or waiting patiently for the wounded to die.'

A great hullabaloo developed over the Sirdar's treatment of the enemy wounded. Winston Churchil expressed his opinion bluntly in print:

> I must personally record that there was a general impression that the fewer the prisoners, the greater would be the satisfaction of the commander … The result was that there were many wounded killed … Nearly all who perished were killed by the Soudanese and Egyptian troops.

However, he also noted that 5000 prisoners were taken. Privately, Churchill told friends that he thought Kitchener's treatment of the wounded was 'disgraceful'.

51. Camp followers were quickly at work looting the dead.

Ernest Bennett stoked the fire by claiming he had seen unarmed dervishes shot down. Questions were asked in Parliament. Most war correspondents defended Kitchener in their publications but Bennett was adamant that

> Our native battalions were soon busily engaged in killing the wounded … a large number of servants and camp-followers were also busy. Some carried clubs or spears, others had managed to secure old rifles … The barbarous usage of killing the wounded has become traditional in Soudanese warfare, and in some cases it must be looked upon as a painful necessity … Still, when all has been said in defence of this practice, it is certain that in many cases wounded Dervishes, unarmed and helpless, were butchered from sheer wantonness and lust of bloodshed.

Kitchener always denied 'the cruel, and to my mind, disgraceful charges' that any of his soldiers 'wantonly killed wounded or unarmed Dervishes,' though he qualified this statement with the words, 'when no longer in a position to do us injury'.

52. A rare photograph of a correspondent (almost certainly Rene Bull) trying to take a picture of a dying dervish (this may even be the same man who rose and chased him).

There were many instances of warriors feigning death or injury, then rising up and attacking British and Egyptian troops. Private Donald Macpherson, Cameron Highlanders, rebutted Kitchener's story by admitting, 'We finished them off and the Soudanese finished them off, too.'

On 3 September, when it had been suggested by some that water and biscuits should be taken out to the wounded, Macpherson claimed there 'was a perfect uproar, next to a riot … they should give each one a round of ammunition.'

Such was the suffering that even Churchill thought the wounded needed either a glass of water or a fast bullet. One or two days after the battle Neville Lyttelton rode past two dervishes who had been shot through both thighs. They were moving along the ground using two sticks to propel themselves. Two days later, three miles further on, and after about 90 hours without food or water he saw the same two men arrive at the British lines.

Churchill found a warrior with his foot blown off who had covered a mile in three days and had two more to go. Thousands must have died through lack of water or medical assistance.

War crimes, at least by twenty-first century standards, definitely took place; the correspondent, Lionel James, claimed he was with Slatin Pasha just after the battle when they found a small boy leading a donkey with a wounded dervish on its back. Recognising the man as Osman Azrak, the Austrian 'drew back his lips like a snarling wolf,' took the stricken Emir off the beast and summoned a passing Sudanese soldier to bayonet him.

Some writers, like Philip Ziegler, dispute whether this could have been Osman who probably died earlier in the day, but it seems unlikely that James made up the whole story (he claimed to have kept the Emir's beads as a souvenir), in which case Slatin may well have killed an unknown Mahdist in cold blood.

Dealing with such vast numbers of enemy wounded was beyond the resources of the British and Egyptian Army doctors, nor did they fall within Lord Cromer's carefully allotted budgets. On 3 September a secret set of orders, sent from Lord Salisbury,

53. 'The aftermath of the Battle of Omdurman'. (H.C.S. Eppings Wright, The Illustrated London News)

were opened by Kitchener. His instructions were to make haste 700 miles further up river to Fashoda and prevent a French expedition from planting its country's flag on the Upper Nile. 'No corpses' was the Prime Minister's pointed request.

AFTER THE BATTLE

Omdurman destroyed the power that was Mahdiism, but did not put an immediate end to the Khalifa, or his supporters. This took fifteen more months, during which period further battles were fought, and men died on both sides.

Kitchener was soon steaming up river to deal with the threat at Fashoda. In negotiations with the friendly French Commandant, Jean-Baptiste Marchand, the Sirdar and Wingate were able to reach a stalemate. Meantime, earnest negotiations between Paris and London led to the French backing down; the Upper Nile would stay in the British sphere of influence.

Pursuit of the Khalifa

Just five days after Omdurman a force of 1300 men, mainly Egyptian Army reservists, under Colonel Parsons RA, set out from Kassala to occupy the headquarters of the Emir Ahmed Fadel, whose 3000 warriors posed a threat between the Abyssinian border and the Blue Nile. The two sides clashed at Gedaref on 22 September. Parsons won the fight (and a final Victoria Cross of the campaign was later awarded to Bimbashi the Honourable A. Hore-Ruthven, who rescued a wounded Egyptian officer under heavy fire), but was trapped there for several weeks.

A BUREAUCRATIC VC

There was a long debate about awarding a Victoria Cross to Hore-Ruthven after the fight at Gedaref. He was officially Absent Without Leave from his militia battalion in Scotland, was below required officer height and had been applying for a regular commission. After a protracted correspondence it took royal intervention to get Hore-Ruthven his medal.

On 26 December 1898, the emir was forced into a battle at Rosaires on the Blue Nile by another Egyptian force led by 'Taffy' Lewis. The Mahdist defeat came at the cost of an infantry assault; some 500 dervishes were slain, 1700 captured, but Lewis lost over 30 men killed and more than 140 officers and men wounded amongst the 10th Sudanese and his tribal irregulars.

Next it was the turn of the Sirdar's brother, Walter Kitchener, to lead an expedition into the blistering wastes of Kordofan. They toiled for two weeks in January 1899, and got to within ten miles of their quarry before it was learned that the Khalifa, far from being supported by 1500–2000 tribesmen, now had with him an ansar of upwards of 8000 dervishes! Walter Kitchener prudently decided to retire before he became a second Hicks.

Um Dibaykarat

For ten months during the hottest part of the year, the British waited and the Khalifa wondered. Then, in November 1899, Reginald Wingate, commanding his first and only expedition, set out with a 3700-strong column, including the 9th and 13th Sudanese battalions, a squadron of cavalry, 6 Camel Corps companies, a field battery and 6 Maxims to settle matters once and for all.

On 22 November they surprised Ahmed Fadel, with a loss of 400 Mahdist dead, though the wily emir escaped. Next morning

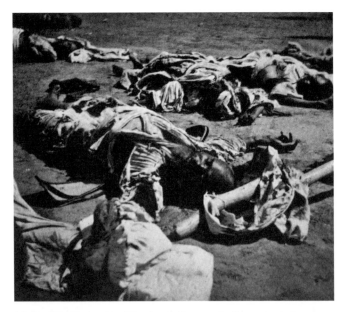

54. Dervish dead at Um Dibaykarat. The man in the centre is the young Emir Ahmed Fadil.

55. The Khalifa Abdullahi lies dead – killed by Maxim fire – at Um Dibaykarat surrounded by his faithful retinue.

a deserter told Wingate that the Khalifa was camped just seven miles away.

In a classic dawn attack on 24 November the Anglo-Egyptians stormed the Mahdist encampment after it had been raked by artillery and Maxim fire. Realising that it was the end, Abdullahi, who was wounded in the left arm, ordered his emirs to dismount, roll out their prayer mats, face Mecca and join him in worship. Ali wad Helu disobeyed and charged into a hail of bullets. Most of the Khalifa's entourage, including Ahmed Fadel, stayed with him to the end and were shot down. One who escaped yet again was the eternally cunning Osman Digna.

Gunner Franks examined the bodies and wrote: 'I went back to see the Khalifa. In front of him lay the riflemen of his bodyguard, in a double line, evidently killed to a man in their places shooting, each man had shot and shot till he died.' A little way beyond lay Abdullahi. He had, thought Franks, 'quite a nice face, a stoutish built, powerful, elderly gentleman, with a slight grey beard … not a bit the cruel tyrant one expected.'

THE LEGACY

Tactical Aspects

Military historian H. Keown-Boyd has described Omdurman as an 'uninteresting' battle tactically because 'on the Mahdist side no generalship was displayed and on the other little required.' The outcome, however, could have been very different, especially if the dervishes had launched a night attack. Without it the Khalifa's fate was probably sealed, though Archibald Hunter also felt that 'If he had surrounded us on three sides first & then charged all together he might have given infinite more trouble.'

The Mahdists failed to secure Jebel Surgham before the battle. This was a mistake, but then Kitchener also missed an opportunity to occupy the hill. Douglas Haig felt the Sirdar ought to have thrown forward his left flank after the Khalifa divided his forces, 'gradually drawing in his right and extending his left southwards', thus cutting off the enemy from Omdurman.

Haig wrote that Kitchener 'seems to have had no plan, or tactical idea', beyond letting the dervishes attack his camp. Most critics reserve their scorn for the Sirdar's behaviour at the start of Phase Two when he let the gap develop between MacDonald's brigade and the rest. Hunter, however, must share in the blame for this error, though Kitchener was clearly impatient to get into the city. His advance, while two armies were still unaccounted for, has been oft-criticised, one historian commenting that 'Thanks to MacDonald's abilities and bravery, Kitchener won the battle of Omdurman.'

The Sirdar's mistakes were small compared to those of the Mahdists who could have compelled the British to fight away from the Nile in the inhospitable desert, or ambushed them in thick scrub, or even defended their capital, street by street. One officer thought that an attack on the city would have cost at least 3000 Anglo-Egyptian lives.

Strategical Aspects

The Sirdar's objective – first to last – was to bring the Mahdists to battle near Omdurman. He fed, watered and transported his troops all the way from Cairo in a superb manner. His personal obsession with details and a failure to delegate (noticeable in the final battle), might have been a disadvantage, but Kitchener kept himself under control, and he achieved it all on the cheap.

Mahdiism was destroyed with a loss of about 1500 Anglo-Egyptian lives, with only 15 per cent battle casualties and at a cost of less than £2.5 million, of which half had been invested in railways. The northern Sudan was made secure, under British control, and the south would soon follow.

Victors

Following the victory Kitchener was made an earl; he became supreme commander in South Africa during the later stages of the Second Boer War 1899–1902. He died when HMS *Hampshire* – on which he was travelling – struck a German mine and sank in 1916 while en route to Russia. MacDonald won more fame in the Boer War but committed suicide in 1903 after allegations of misconduct with schoolboys in Ceylon. Wauchope was killed leading his beloved Highlanders at Magersfontein in 1899. The

56. 'Thank You' – Kitchener is honoured by Britannia in a Punch cartoon.

same war wrecked Gatacre's career and he died in Abyssinia in 1906. Hamilton's career also went into slow decline. The only one of the commanders to emerge from the Boer War untarnished was Lyttelton.

The last remaining Tommy who fought at Omdurman – James Miles, 2nd Battalion, Rifle Brigade – died aged 97 on 20 January 1977. He described the battle, quite pithily, as 'bloody hot!'

Losers

The 1970s saw the deaths of the last Mahdists including Sayyid Musa Ya'qub who was with the Khalifa at Um Dibaykarat. The last emir to die, in 1936, was Yunus al Dikaym, a cruel former governor of Dongola, who stayed by Abdullahi's side at Omdurman and also

FULL FATHOM FIVE

Kitchener found himself in hot water after he allowed Gordon's nephew, Major W. Gordon RE, to blow up the Mahdi's tomb and throw his bones in the river. The skull was sent to the Royal College of Surgeons in London. This act appalled Queen Victoria who had great respect for all rulers, even her enemies, pointing out that the Mahdi, even if 'bad and cruel, after all, was a man of a certain importance'. Lord Cromer, too, thought it an 'unwise' act and had the skull returned to the Sudan and quietly buried in a Muslim cemetery at Wadi Halfa. There it still lies beneath the waters of man-made Lake Nasser.

the final massacre. Osman Digna was finally caught by the British in 1900; he remained an unrepentant Mahdist, but his captivity was gradually made less absolute. In 1924 he was allowed to go on a pilgrimage to Mecca and he died two years later, aged 86.

In August 1899 the third Khalifa, Muhammad Sharif, was executed with two of the Mahdi's sons. The trio had been accused of instigating a revolt on trumped up charges. The Mahdi's family remains influential in the Khartoum region to the present day.

Glory or Shame

In the British psyche the Battle of Omdurman has always been a curious mixture of glory and shame. For all the exploits of the 21st Lancers it is the spectacular dervish charges against massed riflemen that has excited the imagination. Writers, then and now, have been most impressed not with how the British fought, but how the dervishes died.

'It was the last day of Mahdiism, and the greatest,' was how G.W. Steevens described it. Winston Churchill best expressed the shame when he declared, 'there was nothing *dulce et decorum* about the Dervish dead. Nothing of the dignity of unconquerable

THE SUDAN ON SCREEN

The Battle of Omdurman formed the climax of Alexander Korda's celebrated 1939 film *The Four Feathers*. The battle is reduced to a spectacular camel charge, but the release of the prisoners, along with evocative shots of steamers being hauled over the cataracts and a very realistic Kitchener, make it unmissable. The same scenes were re-edited into the 1955 remake, *Storm over the Nile*. Seventeen years later Richard Attenborough directed *Young Winston*. This has the petite John Mills as a most unreal Sirdar along with a voiceover that states that the famous 21st charge took place on the day after the battle! At least the charge itself is thrilling and gives some idea of what it must have felt like.

manhood. All was filthy corruption. Yet these were as brave men as ever walked the earth.' Steevens wrote the best and final epitaph on the battle: 'Our men were perfect, but the Dervishes were superb – beyond perfection. It was the largest, best and bravest army that ever fought against us for Mahdiism, and it died worthily of the huge empire that Mahdiism won and kept so long.'

ORDERS OF BATTLE

British Forces

Major-General H.H. Kitchener, Sirdar of the Egyptian Army

British Infantry Division (Gatacre)

1st Brigade (Wauchope): 1st Royal Warwickshire Regiment (Jones); 1st Lincolnshire Regiment (Louth); 1st Seaforth Highlanders (Murray); 1st Cameron Highlanders (G. Money); 6 Maxim guns manned by 16 Co. Eastern Division Royal Artillery; 1 detachment Royal Engineers.
2nd Brigade (Lyttelton): 1st Grenadier Guards (Hatton); 1st Northumberland Fusiliers (C. Money); 2nd Lancashire Fusiliers (Collinwood); 2nd Rifle Brigade (Hayward); 4 Maxim guns manned by Royal Irish Fusiliers; 1 detachment Royal Engineers

Egyptian Division (Hunter)

1st Brigade (MacDonald): 2nd Egyptians (Pink); 9th Sudanese (Walter); 10th Sudanese (Nason); 11th Sudanese (Jackson)
2nd Brigade (Maxwell): 8th Egyptians (Kiloussi Bey); 12th Sudanese (Townshend); 13th Sudanese (Smith-Dorrien); 14th Sudanese (Shekleton)

3rd Brigade (Lewis): 3rd Egyptians (Sillern); 4th Egyptians (Sparkes); 7th Egyptians (Fateh Bey); 15th Egyptians (Hickman)
4th Brigade (Collinson): 1st Egyptians (Doran); 5th Egyptians (Burhan Bey); 17th Sudanese (Bunberry); 18th Sudanese (Matchett); Cavalry (Burn-Murdoch)
Cavalry: 21st Lancers (Martin); Egyptian Cavalry (Broadwood); Camel Corps (Tudway)
Artillery (Long): 32nd Field Battery Royal Artillery (8 guns); 37th Field Battery Royal Artillery (6.5 in howitzers); 1st Egyptian Hortse Battery (6 6cm Krupp guns 2 Maxims); 2nd, 3rd, 4th, 5th Egyptian Field Batteries (each 6 Maxim-Nordenfeldts + 2 Maxims)

Naval Forces (Keppel)

3 1889-class armoured screw gunboats (each with 2 Nordenfeldt guns, 1 q/f 12-pdr, 1 howitzer, 4 Maxim guns); 3 1896 armounred sternwheel gunboats (each with 1 q/f 12-pdr, 2 6-pdrs, 4 Maxim guns); 4 old class armoured sternwheel gunboats (each with 1 12-pdr, 2 Maxim-Nordenfelft guns)

Total strength: 8200 British, 17,600 Egyptian/Sudanese troops

Mahdist Forces

Khalifa Abdullahi-al-Taishi

Dark Green Flag (Uthman al-Din): Khalifa's bodyguard; Uthman al-Din's bodyguard; 16 rubs commanded by 9 Ta'aisha emirs, 2 Abyssinian emirs and 5 others; 2900 horse, 12,900 rifles, 1 'French' gun, 1 mountain gun, 1 Remington machine gun.
Black Flag (Al-Rayya Al-Zarqua) (Ya'qub): various tribal groups including Ta'aisha (Othman wad-al-Dikaim) and Humur (Muslim Isa); also Habbaniya, Rizauqat, Bani Halba, Baggara, Kababish, Danaqla, Ja'allyin tribes; 1600 horse; 1450 rifles; 1 Krupp gun and 1 Nordenfeldt gun.

Green Flag (Al Rayya Al- Khadra) (Khalifa Ali wad-Helu): 3 rubs of White Nile tribes commanded by emirs Digham, al-lihawin and Kinana; 800 horse, unknown number of firearms.

Emir Osman Digna (no Flag, his being captured at Tamai in 1884); personal bodyguard of 9 rubs under 9 emirs; 190 horse; 350 rifles.

Red Flag (Al-Rayya Al-Hamra) (Khalifa al-Sharif): 81 men

Emir Osman Azrak: personal bodyguard 81 men

Total strength: approximately 45,000 men

FURTHER READING

Alford, Lieutenant H., and Sword, Lieutenant W., *The Egyptian Soudan: Its Loss And Recovery* (London, 1898)

Anglesey, Marquess of, *A History Of The British Cavalry, 1872–1898* (London, 1982)

Arthur, Sir G., *Life of Lord Kitchener* (London, 1920)

_____ *General Sir John Maxwell* (London, 1932)

Asher, M., *Khartoum The Ultimate Imperial Adventure* (London, 2005)

Atteridge, A., *Towards Khartoum: The Story of The Soudan War of 1896* (London, 1897)

_____ *Wars of the 'Nineties: A History of The Warfare of the Last Ten Years of The Nineteenth Century* (London, 1899)

Barthorp, M., *War on the Nile: Britain, Egypt and the Sudan 1882–1898* (Poole, 1984)

_____ and Turner, P., *The British Army On Campaign 4 1882–1902* (London, 1988)

Bedri, B., *Memoirs* (Oxford, 1969)

Bennett, E., *The Downfall of the Dervishes Being A Sketch of the Final Sudan Campaign Of 1898* (London, 1898)

Bond, B., ed. *Victorian Military Campaigns* (London, 1967)

Brighton, T., *The Last Charge: The 21st Lancers and the Battle of Omdurman* (Ramsbury, 1998)

Brook-Shepherd, G., *Between Two Flags: The Life Of Baron Sir Rudolph von Slatin Pasha* (New York, 1973)

Burleigh, B., *Sirdar And Khalifa: Or the Re-Conquest of the Soudan* (London, 1898)

_____ *Khartoum Campaign: Or the Re-Conquest of the Soudan* (London, 1899)

Butler, Lieutenant-General Sir W., *An Autobiography* (London, 1911)

Churchill, R., *Winston S. Churchill: Volume 1 Companion Part 2, 1896–1900* (London, 1967)

Churchill, W., *The River War: An Historical Account Of The Re-Conquest Of The Sudan* (London, 1899)

_____ *My Early Life* (London, 1930)

Corvi, S., and Beckett, I. (ed.) *Victoria's Generals* (Barnsley, 2009)

Creagh, Sir O., and Humphris, E., *The Victoria Cross 1856–1920* (Polstead 1985)

Cromer, Earl of., *Modern Egypt* (London, 1908)

Doolittle, D., *A Soldier's Hero: General Sir Archibald Hunter* (Narrangansett, 1991)

Douglas, Sir G., *The Life Of Major-General Wauchope* (London, 1904)

Emery, F., *Marching Over Africa: Letters from Victorian Soldiers* (London, 1986)

Farwell, B., *Prisoners of the Mahdi: The Story of the Mahdist Revolt from the Fall of Khartoum to the Reconquest of the Sudan By Kitchener Fourteen Years Later, and of the Daily Sufferings in Captivity of Three European Prisoners, A Soldier, A Merchant And A Priest* (London, 1967)

_____ *Queen Victoria's Little Wars* (London, 1972)

_____ *Eminent Victorian Soldiers: Seekers of Glory* (London, 1986)

Featherstone, D., *Victoria's Enemies: An A-Z of Colonial Warfare* (London, 1989)

_____ *Khartoum 1885: General Gordon's Last Stand* (London, 1993)

_____ *Omdurman 1898: Kitchener's Victory in the Sudan* (London, 1993)

Fortescue-Brickdale, Sir C., ed. *Major-General Sir Henry Hallam-Parr* (London, 1917)

Gatacre, B., *General Gatacre: The Story of the Life and Services of Sir William Forbes Gatacre* (London, 1906)

Green, D., *Armies Of God: Islam And Empire on the Nile, 1869–1899* (London, 2007)

Grenfell, Lord F.M., *Memoirs* (London, 1925)

Haggard, A., *Under Crescent and Star* (Edinburgh, 1896)

Harrington, P. and Sharf, F., *Omdurman 1898: The Eye-Witnesses Speak* (London, 1998)

Holt, P., *The Mahdist State In The Sudan 1881–1898* (Oxford, 1958)

Hunter, A., *Kitchener's Sword-Arm: The Life and Campaigns of General Sir Archibald Hunter* (Staplehurst, 1996)

Jackson, H., *Osman Digna* (London, 1926)

James, Colonel L., *High Pressure: Being Some Record of Activities in the Service of the Times Newspaper* (London, 1929)

James, L., *The Savage Wars: British Campaigns In Africa, 1870–1920* (New York, 1985)

Keown-Boyd, H., *A Good Dusting: A Centenary Review of the Sudan Campaigns 1883–1899* (London, 1986)

_____ *Soldiers of the Nile: A Biographical History of the British Officers of the Egyptian Army 1882–1925* (Thornbury, 1996)

Knight, E., *Letters from the Sudan* (London, 1897)

Knight, I., and Scollins, R., *Queen Victoria's Enemies* (London, 1989)

_____ *Marching to the Drums: Eye-Witness Accounts of War from the Kabul Massacre to the Siege of Mafeking* (London, 1999)

Lewis, D., *The Race to Fashoda: European Colonialism and African Resistance in the Scramble for Africa* (New York, 1987)

Longford, E., *Victoria R.I.* (London, 1964)

Lyttelton, General Sir N., *Eighty Years: Soldiering, Politics, Games* (London, 1928)

MacLaren, R., *Canadians on the Nile, 1882–1898* (Vancouver, 1978)

Magnus, P., *Kitchener: Portrait Of An Imperialist* (New York, 1958)

Manning, S., *Evelyn Wood V.C. Pillar of Empire* (Barnsley, 2007)

Manchester, W., *The Last Lion: Winston Spencer Churchill* (New York, 1973)

Maxse, Colonel F., *Seymour Vandaleur: Lieutenant-Colonel, Scots Guards and Irish Guards* (London, 1906)

Meredith, J., ed. *Omdurman Diaries 1898* (London, 1998)

Moorehead, A., *The White Nile* (London, 1960)

Neillands, R., *The Dervish Wars: Gordon and Kitchener in the Sudan, 1880–1898* (London, 1996)

Nicoll, F., *The Sword Of The Prophet: The Mahdi of the Sudan and the Death of General Gordon* (Thrupp, 2004)

Neufeld, C., *A Prisoner of the Khaleefa: Twelve Years' Captivity at Omdurman* (New York, 1899)

Pollock, J., *Kitchener: The Road to Omdurman* (London, 1998)

Pritchard, Lieutenant H., *Sudan Campaign 1896–1899* (London, 1899)

Roberts, A., *Salisbury: Victorian Titan* (London, 1999)

Robinson, R., Gallagher, J. and Denny, A., *Africa and the Victorians: The Official Mind of Imperialism* (London, 1961)

Royle, C., *The Egyptian Campaigns 1882 to 1885: New and Revised Edition Continued to December, 1899* (London, 1900)

Royle, T., *Death Before Dishonour: The True Story Of Fighting Mac* (New York, 1982)

Russell, D., *Winston Churchill Soldier: The Military Life Of A Gentleman At War* (London, 2005)

Sanderson, G., *England, Europe and the Upper Nile 1882–1899* (Edinburgh, 1965)

Sandes, Lieutenant-Colonel E., *The Royal Engineers in Egypt and the Sudan* (Chatham, 1937)

Scott, D. (ed.) *Douglas Haig: The Preparatory Prologue 1861–1914* (Barnsley, 2006)

Scudamore, F., *A Sheaf of Memories* (London, 1925)

Settle, J., *Anecdotes of Soldiers: In Peace and War* (London, 1905)

Shibeika, M., *British Policy in the Sudan 1882–1902* (Oxford, 1952)

Sherson, E., *Townshend of Chitral and Kut* (London, 1928)

Slatin, R., *Fire and Sword in the Sudan: A Personal Narrative of Fighting and Serving The Dervishes 1879–1895* (London, 1896)

Smith-Dorrien, General Sir H., *Memories of Forty-Eight Years Service* (London, 1925)

Spiers, E., *Sudan: The Reconquest Reappraised* (London, 1998)

_____ *The Scottish Soldier And Empire 1854–1902* (Edinburgh, 2006)

Steevens, G., *With Kitchener to Khartum* (Edinburgh, 1898)

Symons, J., *England's Pride: The Story of the Gordon Relief Expedition* (London, 1965)

Theobald, A., *The Mahdiya: A History of the Anglo-Egyptian Sudan 1881–1899* (London, 1967)

Uzoigwe, G., *Britain and the Conquest Of Africa: The Age of Salisbury* (Ann Arbor, 1974)

Warner, P., *Dervish: The Rise and Fall of an African Empire* (London, 1973)

Watkins, O., *With Kitchener's Army: Being a Chaplain's Experiences with the Nile Expedition, 1898* (London, 1898)

Watson, Colonel Sir C., *The Life Of Major-General Sir Charles William Wilson Royal Engineers* (London, 1909)

Wilkinson-Latham, R., *The Sudan Campaigns 1881–1898* (London, 1976)

_____ *From Our Special Correspondent: Victorian War Correspondents and their Campaigns* (London, 1979)

Wilson, Colonel Sir C., *From Korti to Khartum: A Journal of the Desert March from Korti to Gubat and of the Ascent of the Nile in General Gordon's Steamers* (Edinburgh, 1886)

Wingate, Major F., *Mahdiism and the Egyptian Soudan: Being an Account of the Rise and Progress of Mahdiism, and of Subsequent Events in the Soudan to the Present Time* (London, 1891)

Wood, F.M. Sir E., *From Mid-Shipman to Field-Marshal* (London, 1906.

Woods, F., ed. *Young Winston's Wars: The Original Despatches of*

Winston S. Churchill, War Correspondent 1897–1900 (London, 1972)

Wright, W., *A Tidy Little War: The British Invasion of Egypt, 1882* (Brimscombe Port, 2009)

Ziegler, P., *Omdurman* (London, 1973)

Zulfo, I., *Karari: The Sudanese Account of the Battle of Omdurman* (London, 1980)

*57. 'Death of a gallant officer in the Soudan.' (*The Illustrated London News*)*

INDEX

EXPLORE HISTORY'S MAJOR CONFLICTS WITH
BATTLE STORY